Start Up Your Fashion Label

AARTHI GUNNUPURI has worked as an advertising copywriter and a freelance journalist. Her articles have appeared in several publications, including *Femina, Marie Claire, Vogue, Outlook, Hindustan Times, Prevention, Yahoo* and CNN.com. She has also reported from the UN Headquarters in New York, and holds a degree in Media, Communication and Development from the London School of Economics. This is her first book.

GW00746294

Start Up YOUR FASHION LABEL

AARTHI GUNNUPURI

COLLINS BUSINESS
An Imprint of HarperCollins Publishers

First published in India in 2016 by Collins Business
An imprint of HarperCollins *Publishers* India

Copyright © Aarthi Gunnupuri 2016

P-ISBN: 978-93-5177-935-3
E-ISBN: 978-93-5177-936-0

2 4 6 8 10 9 7 5 3 1

Aarthi Gunnupuri asserts the moral right
to be identified as the author of this work.

The views and opinions expressed in this book are the author's own
and the facts are as reported by her, and the publishers are not
in any way liable for the same.

HarperCollins *Publishers*
A-75, Sector 57, Noida, Uttar Pradesh 201301, India
1 London Bridge Street, London, SE1 9GF, United Kingdom
Hazelton Lanes, 55 Avenue Road, Suite 2900, Toronto, Ontario M5R 3L2
and 1995 Markham Road, Scarborough, Ontario M1B 5M8, Canada
25 Ryde Road, Pymble, Sydney, NSW 2073, Australia
195 Broadway, New York, NY 10007, USA

Typeset in 11/14 Requiem at
Manipal Digital Systems, Manipal

Printed and bound at
Thomson Press (India) Ltd.

To my son Dhruva,
at the beginning of a very exciting journey

Contents

Smart Ways to Use the Book

1. Explore!

Most chapters in this book feature 'Explore!' notes. Use them to explore websites and links on the web to understand a particular subject or theme better. Every 'Explore!' note comes with instructions on how to find relevant web pages, videos, images, or related material.

2. Do it!

Often 'Explore!' notes are followed by 'Do it!' notes. These notes offer stimulating ideas to put into action so that you're not just reading but actually doing something to realize your dream of becoming a designer and entrepreneur. Following these 'Do it!' notes will result in concrete, helpful output, such as a fashion journal, a portfolio, or a textile swatchbook, to name a few.

At the end of the book, you will find a curated collection of the 'Explore!' and 'Do it!' notes under their respective chapter headings as well. Just get back to the last section when you're in the mood to check out some 'Explore!' links or feel like doing some exercises.

3. Action Plan

Towards the end of many of the chapters you will find an 'Action Plan' that will help translate your newly acquired knowledge into actually setting up a fashion business. Follow the 'Action Plan' and you will be taking firm steps towards having your own fashion label.

4. Inspiration

Most chapters have 'Inspiration' sections towards the end, where designers talk about how they tackled a specific area during their journey towards becoming a fashion entrepreneur. Read, enjoy and get inspired.

INTRODUCTION

Glitzy photo shoots, glossy centrespreads and that glorious moment in a fashion show when models line up and the designer takes a bow – thoughts like these can give goosebumps to an aspiring designer. Whether becoming a fashion designer seems like a sweet but far-fetched goal, or you've convinced yourself that you can be India's next Armani or Chanel, this book can take you closer to your take-a-bow moment. But before that...

Who Is a Fashion Entrepreneur?

A few examples: Armani, Chanel, Louis Vuitton, Dolce & Gabbana, Satya Paul, Sabyasachi, JJ Valaya, Anita Dongre. The common strand that binds most famous labels is the spirit of the entrepreneur. Almost every famous fashion label is the dream-child of a designer turned designer-entrepreneur.

This book is not just a guide to that world. It's also meant to be your personal cheerleader, inspiring you with real-life stories of designer-entrepreneurs and their journeys. There are a wide range of conversations within these pages, from those with designers just starting out, to those who've made it: JJ Valaya, Anita Dongre, Tanya Sharma, Chaitanya Rao and Elina Ahluwalia, to name a few.

You'll find their tips and advice throughout this book, as well as a lot of practical information to help you to achieve your goals. In thinking of this book, we've tried to cover a whole range of questions:

Do I need to be able to draw to become a fashion designer? (Chapter 1)

What is a business plan? How do I launch my business? (Chapter 2)

How do I register my brand name? (Chapter 3)

How do I market my brand with little or no money? (Chapter 5)

What does the manufacturing process of a big label look like? How can I launch my first collection? (Chapter 6)

What is a fashion week? How can I show at famous events like the Lakme Fashion Week? (Chapter 9)

At the end of this book, you will find you have more answers and fewer questions, and on the way you will find information that can fuel your talent. What you know is more important than who you know in today's world, and even India is slowly but surely bidding goodbye to the days when connections or inheritances mattered. As a famous YouTube video says: '*Mera baap kaun hain tu nahin janta* ... but you will know me!'

Before we go any further, let's clear up one potential misunderstanding: this book will *not* teach you how to design. Designing is just the tip of the iceberg. Being a fashion designer also means embracing ten other roles, such as those of entrepreneur, marketing manager and trend spotter.

That being said, take a deep breath and read on. It's not as hard as it sounds, and I will take you through as much of it as possible.

This book has been written exclusively for the Indian reader. The designers interviewed, the research and the context are all Indian. A practical, business-oriented approach works for us security-minded Indians. At the same time, the emphasis on entrepreneurship also caters to our growing desire to be independent and not limit our success to job promotions or monthly pay cheques.

The time is ripe to 'Make in India'. Make your label in India. Make it big in India. And then take on the world! In the last two decades, Indian designers have used the country's burgeoning fashion industry as a launch pad to global fame. Katy Perry has been spotted in a Manish Arora outfit, Lady Gaga has collected outfits by designer duo Alpana & Neeraj, and style-icon Sarah Jessica Parker favours Suneet Verma's clutches.

Even Indian-born designers based in the US, like Saloni Lodha and Naeem Khan, are building towering global reputations. Naeem Khan, who moved to the US at the age of twenty, shot to fame after Michelle Obama wore the designer's strapless metallic gown for a state dinner at the White House. Saloni Lodha graduated from Sophia Polytechnic in Mumbai and set up a UK-based eponymous brand sported by the likes of Naomi Watts and Emma Watson. If they can do it, so can you – one step at a time. How about starting off by selling at one of the many retail stores in India? Walk through a Lifestyle or Shoppers Stop store and you'll find home-grown brands like AND and W jostling for space (and standing out!) with international pret names like Vero Moda and Zara. The time is right for young, talented designers and all you need is know what to do and how to go about things. And this book is here to help you.

And in case I gave you the impression that it's going to be easy, it's not, but this book will hopefully be the start of a long, fruitful journey. May you become a fashion designer and entrepreneur. And while not everybody becomes famous, may you be one of the chosen few. Good luck!

1

BECOME A MASTER OF FASHION DESIGN

Successful fashion entrepreneurs are masters of design. You too can master the design process. However, there's no single path to becoming a good fashion designer. Some start by enrolling in a tailoring course while others join an expensive fashion institute; some decide to intern with an established designer and yet others decide to just wing it. You have to choose a path that's most appropriate for you. There are enough stories from fashion designers in this book to inspire you, but the final path you choose will have to be yours.

Maybe you're eighteen and have decided that you have the time to go to a fashion school. Good for you. But what if you're a mother of two and dread going back to college? Or you're a marketing analyst looking for a career change? How can you 'learn' to become a fashion designer? Let's start where every fashion designer's journey begins – the drawing board.

ALL ABOUT FASHION ILLUSTRATION

Without further ado, let's address a question that many bright and creative future designers may be wrestling with: Do I need to be able to draw to become a fashion designer? The real answer lies somewhere between yes and no. Yes, you need to be able to articulate your design idea on paper. At the very least, enough to help your tailoring team understand what to do. But, no, you don't need to be Pablo Picasso or MF Hussain to become a Coco Chanel or Rohit Bal.

Let's elaborate. Reputed national and international fashion schools are flooded with applications from keen young people. The institutions, therefore, lay out a whole bunch of 'prerequisites' that make their admissions processes competitive, and, let's be honest, stressful. Typically, the ability to draw is one of those so-called 'prerequisites'. This is to be reflected in the students' samples or portfolio book as part of their fashion design school application.

Many prospective students spend hours trying to perfect their drawing skills in the hope of getting into these schools. In the world of work, however, a mastery of fashion illustration or drawing is not necessary to begin your career. 'Begin' being the operative word here. What this means, essentially, is that you don't have to wait to perfect your drawing abilities to kick-start your fashion designing career. Have some ideas? Start putting them down on paper. Practice will help; being able to do the basic sketches that take a design from dream to reality is a necessary skill for an independent fashion designer, particularly for those just starting out.

ABOUT DRAWING: EXPERT SPEAK

Chandigarh-based fashion entrepreneur Sohni Makkar has been running a successful local brand, 'Sohni', for close to two decades now. Long before brands like Fabindia made inroads into smaller cities like Chandigarh, Sohni was catering to local fashionistas who were looking for chic but down-to-earth Indian wear, made from local textiles and weaves. As an independent fashion entrepreneur, here's what she has to say about the importance of the ability to draw.

'Highly stylized fashion illustrations do look glamorous but in my opinion, they are mostly marketing tools. They are like illustrated advertisements for your designs. You need to be able to do some basic drawing, enough to get the proportions right – like the armhole size has to be relative to the size of the shirt,' she says.

As an entrepreneur, you have more freedom during the design process. If you can do some basic drawing with the right proportions, you should be fine. But what if your circumstances change? You may decide to join a reputed fashion house or collaborate with a label. The design team there may be keen on seeing a portfolio that demonstrates a good grasp over drawing the human body, sketching interesting designs in an appealing manner, understanding human proportions, etc. Or, your business may take off and you may need to hire a number of junior designers and interns. You will not wish to see sloppy drawing work from them, and this means leading by example.

The last word on the matter: It is not necessary to be a master, but practise your drawing to make sure that weak drawing skills don't hold you back from your goals.

DO IT!

- You may choose to start a scrapbook (or any book where you put together pieces of relevant information, pictures and ideas). Start collecting information, write down tips you come across, and practise your drawing skills. Several experts, amateurs and students share tricks and tips related to the art of fashion illustration on YouTube and various blogs, like thefashionillustrator.com, sabinepieper.com, hand.fashionary.org, etc.
- Pinterest is another site that can give you a great deal of exposure to this art form. Take printouts of illustrations you like and paste them in your book.
- You can also go to Amazon.in and find several books on fashion illustrations published by famous designers. You can use the 'Look Inside' option on the website to check out sections of the book before buying.

QUALITIES FOR FASHION DESIGN SUCCESS

Before getting too deeply into the nitty-gritty of becoming a fashion designer – and the several areas that will need your attention, including branding, marketing, manufacturing and so on – let's take a brief detour. There are a few, more exciting aspects of being a fashion designer; the intangible qualities and the special 'somethings' that make a fashion designer successful.

Creativity

Often mentioned but difficult to describe, many people have attempted to fit this quality into the neat boundaries of definition, but have failed to do a good job of it. Creativity defies explanation, and yet we know it exists. We know it when we see it. It could be found in a film that moves us in ways we never thought possible, or in a poem that stays with us, or even in an outfit we see on a celebrity and know that we must have. We all come to creativity in our own way. Some have the gift of performance, some are great writers and others are mathematical geniuses.

In the context of fashion design, creativity is tapping your imagination for interesting ideas and translating them into unique and beautiful clothes. But that is a dry, incomplete explanation, because creativity is spectacularly personal. It is different for different designers. This 'personal' aspect of creativity is what gives a brand its uniqueness. How are we able to tell a Ferragamo from a Fendi, or a Ritu Beri from a Ritu Kumar? It is who you are that will make your brand creative.

Did you know that ace-designer JJ Valaya is also a talented artist and photographer? As a multi-faceted person, here's what he has to say: 'A great architect could become a fashion designer. A scientist could become a great designer. Great designers could become great architects, great writers ... creativity is a magical playground. You have to stop building boundaries around yourself. It's different for each person and there are no fixed rules. You have to go to the place that gives you joy.'

EXPLORE!

Nicole Kidman, Julia Roberts and Natalie Portman are just a few of the fans of New York-based fashion designer Isaac Mizrahi's designs. Mizrahi's career as a fashion entrepreneur has had many ups and downs, but one thing nobody questions is the designer's creative genius. Check out Isaac Mizrahi's talk on creativity on the TED Talks website. Many budding fashion designers have found it inspiring.

Originality (Finding Your Signature Style)

Originality is not an abstract, up-in-the-air idea when it comes to this business. In fact, it makes complete business sense. It is very important for fashion designers to be original. In an extremely competitive field like this, the ability to stand out will define your path to success. Putting out ideas and designs like no other will help you earn the loyalty of your clientele and praise from the industry and the media. More importantly, originality will ensure that you don't get sued! (Yes, fashion designers routinely get legal notices, although the legalities surrounding copyright in the fashion industry are still being tested the world over.)

In the era of social media, instant news and a globalized business world, the ability to design independently and be consistently original is of the utmost importance. Even if you don't get sued, the tag 'unoriginal' is not something you want to be associated with. Originality may take a lot of work and exploration. You may find that coming up with original ideas as a matter of routine is not as easy as it seems, and as you get deeper into the field, you will start to feel that much of what seemed original has been done before. But keep at it and you may stumble upon your 'signature style'.

Inspiration

If you had a regular Indian upbringing and went to school and college in India, you will understand the emphasis (or overemphasis) that our society places on academics. We respect education, and that's a good thing, but a well-rounded personality is a huge asset in creative fields. If your parents or other family members encouraged you to draw, read fiction, watch movies and took you to museums, kudos to them. You will already, no doubt, have many points of inspiration. For example, you may have seen the legendary Japanese film-maker Akira Kurosawa's films with your dad as a teenager; if so, perhaps you could use the inspiration of Japanese couture to create an original fashion line! Inspiration can come from anywhere, and the wider your net of ideas, the more interesting, original and creative you can be.

Designer Anita Dongre says: 'As a child, I used to spend a lot of time in my grandmother's house in Jaipur, and was completely enamoured by the beauty of Rajasthan, the colourful markets, the architecture, and the people.' Anita says her childhood in Jaipur inspired her creativity and interest in design. Today, her design choices are also inspired by her personal beliefs and ethics. 'I am a vegan and a PETA supporter, and thus, none of my creations use leather. In fact, I strongly believe in using organic and natural fabrics, which is seen in most of the creations, for my signature label Anita Dongre.'

Domenico Dolce and Stefano Gabbana (of Dolce & Gabbana fame for the newly initiated!) are crazy about old Italian movies. They often credit those movies for their own unique design sensibility.

So what are your interests other than clothes and fashion? Watching TV shows, cooking, reading, photography, a love for animals? It can be absolutely anything. Cultivate your interests, and use them as inspiration for your designs.

Tailoring Skills

After drawing, the second question most novices need to think about involves the practical aspects: sewing, cutting patterns and the other steps in making an outfit. Thankfully, India has a long tradition of tailoring. It's easy to find tailors in most neighbourhoods. Malls and shops that sell ready-made outfits are relatively new. In Europe, where tailoring services are expensive, many newbie designers start off by sewing their own designs.

Many fashion design schools, both in India and abroad, impart basic sewing skills to their students. Aspiring designers will find it helpful to learn the aspects of tailoring, from cutting patterns and sourcing fabrics to adding embellishments to outfits, etc. Once again, like drawing, don't wait to master tailoring before kick-starting your design career. You can start with the basic skills and fine-tune them after you start your label.

However, what you must keep in mind is that sewing skills are essential. Chandigarh-based systems analyst-turned-designer Sohni Makkar has led her successful eponymous label for over fifteen years now. Now, at forty-six, Sohni talks with some pride about belonging to a generation that valued a range of skills. 'During my summer vacations in college, my mother sent me off to a tailoring school. The ability to tailor got better with time and, when I branched off into fashion designing, it really came handy,' she says. Her expert advice to aspiring young designers who grew up in the satellite TV-Internet era is to take up short tailoring courses. Sohni says, without the knowledge of basic tailoring, you will be at a 'serious disadvantage' as a designer.

Other designers like Chennai-based Chaitanya Rao started their careers in fashion designing by taking tailoring courses. 'After high school, I took a year-long tailoring course from a Thai lady. She had a great knowledge of cuts and silhouettes of Western clothes, which not many tailors in India were familiar with at the time. That was the starting point of my career as a fashion designer,' says Rao, who never attended fashion school but is an established designer today.

YOUR FASHION JOURNAL, PORTFOLIO AND FIRST LINE

No matter which stage of designing you are in, whether as an amateur or an established fashion genius, you will always be at work on your portfolio. Let's not forget that fashion trends change every season and almost certainly every year. You will wish to have a long career, which will also be demanding, to be fed with new designs and ideas almost every week. Although this book does not offer comprehensive training in becoming a fashion designer, we will skim over the basics of putting your first portfolio together. But first let's talk about the fashion journal, also known as a creative sketchbook.

What Is a Fashion Journal?

In simple words, a fashion journal is a book that contains all the things that inspire you. It is also known by other names such as the fashion sketchbook, creative journal, etc. Basically, it's a book that can contain samples of fabrics, pictures of embellishments you like, the early stages of designs you intend to make, quotes, poetry, film pictures ... absolutely anything that inspires you.

The fashion journal ties in nicely with some of the qualities we've outlined in the section 'Qualities for Fashion Design Success'. This includes originality, creativity and inspiration. You can use this as a springboard for your journal. Include examples of what you think are truly 'original fashion ideas', jot down any creative ideas you may want to execute later, and include pictures or anything else that you consider to be sources of inspiration.

The fashion journal is the foundation for your portfolio (we will discuss more about the portfolio). The more pictures, notes, sketches and points of inspiration you have in there, the more likely you will conceptualize original designs.

EXPLORE!

With over a lakh views, user xxxhey2's thirty-minute video on 'Example Art Portfolio for Entry into Fashion Design Degree' has to be the most watched YouTube video on the subject of creating a fashion journal. When you watch the video, check out the related videos on fashion sketchbooks on the right-hand tab. Also, read the comments and discussions under the videos on the subject for more information and a better understanding.

DO IT!

Buy a simple blank sheet book. In the first three pages, note down quotes that you find inspiring. In the next three pages, paste magazine cuttings or printouts of your favourite designer outfits. In the next three pages, paste images, quotes or notes on a non-fashion source of inspiration – it could be related to your favourite book, TV show, hobby such as travelling, anything that you find inspiring but with no direct connection to fashion. There, you've started off on your first fashion journal!

Your First Fashion Portfolio

This is an exhaustive area and is typically the culmination of many months, even years of hard work. However, with a little effort you will be able to come out with your own portfolio of designs. A few weeks of maintaining a fashion journal could give you ideas for a theme or a collection. You have to build on that by putting together a bunch of designs; either for a particular season or theme or even a whole lot of 'just like that' designs that share a common thread. You could even pick a genre that you want your first portfolio collection to belong to – lingerie, ethnic wear, men's casuals, women's western wear, etc.

If you want a job or an internship at a fashion house before you set up your fashion label, you may have to invest a lot of time into your portfolio. Sekuzo Sovenyi, a twenty-four-year-old fashion designer, graduated from the National Institute of Fashion Technology in Guwahati and moved back to his hometown of Dimapur in Nagaland to start his own label.

When asked why he didn't join a fashion label in a big city like Delhi or Mumbai, he said he didn't have a portfolio!

'To join big fashion houses you need a professional portfolio book with your collection. Towards the end of my fashion design course, while we did put together a final show, we were given the option of working on our portfolio book after graduation. I simply didn't do it! Not sure if it was the lack of motivation or an interest to be my own boss, in which case one doesn't really need a finished portfolio,' he says. Sekuzo put together a small collection of his designs to sell over social media.

If you plan to do something similar, your portfolio is just part of your plan and you may want to focus more on getting those designs out than spending months creating a finished portfolio.

EXPLORE!

On last count, Amazon.in had close to 300 books on putting together a fashion portfolio. On the homepage, go to the search box, select 'books' instead of 'all' and type 'fashion portfolio' .You will get your results, many of which will have the 'Look Inside' option. This lets you see a few chapters from the book without having to buy it. Enjoy a free preview of books and get more helpful tips on creating your portfolio!

Putting a Portfolio Together: Three Easy Steps for Beginners

So how can an absolute novice with no connections in the fashion industry get a good handle on putting together their first portfolio collection?

1. You can put together a mini portfolio, say of five designs, and reach out to an upcoming fashion designer in your city, or in a city close by. Talented fashion designers are located everywhere in India these days! Meet the designer if possible, and take feedback on your work and tips on how to put your portfolio together.

2. Facebook! You're on Facebook, like, all the time, right? (Just joking!) How about reaching out to a fashion designer on Facebook, and sharing your mini portfolio with them to get feedback? Ask them politely if they'll take a look at your designs before sending off your portfolio.

3. Invest in a good book that focuses exclusively on helping you put together a fashion portfolio. (Check out the Explore! Section on page 12)

INSPIRATION — SOHNI MAKKAR, CHANDIGARH

The label Sohni may not be nationally famous, but women in Chandigarh and neighbouring cities can tell a 'Sohni' from a mile away. Traditional Indian salwars and kurtas find new life in Sohni's designs, as do authentic Indian fabrics and textiles. Sohni Makkar's path epitomizes a working designer's career. It is defined by slow, steady growth and success that seems truly well-deserved. Not every aspiring designer can become a Sabyasachi or Satya Paul overnight but with the right mix of talent and determination, most can achieve what Sohni has – a niche for herself in a space cluttered with an equal mix of wannabes and superstars.

'I worked as a systems analyst at a big multinational pharma company and there was this desire to break free and do something creative. The birth of my first child gave me the push to break from the corporate world and design clothes. I could sew, draw and, having travelled all over the country as an Army kid, had a knack for choosing the best fabrics. I was thirty-one at the time, not young but not too old either. I started with minimal investment in a counter to cut and mark the fabrics and an expert tailor who could both cut and stitch. At the first exhibition and sale I held in the city, my first collection of forty-odd salwar kameez sets just flew off the counters in a couple of days and I knew I was onto something – a career as a fashion designer and entrepreneur.'

FOUR-POINT ACTION PLAN

1. Learn Tailoring

Join a tailoring course, since this is an important skill and helps in properly communicating with and working with your tailors. You will be unable to correct their mistakes, guide them, or offer input to enhance their work without having learned the skill yourself. If you live in a city where such courses are hard to come by, consider investing in a basic sewing machine – the ones with the foot pedal, not the stapler style ones! Watch YouTube videos, read instructions online, or buy a book on tailoring and start practising.

2. Acquire Basic Drawing Skills

If you're a great artist, congratulations! This can only be an asset for your design career. However, if you can't draw, focus on getting your proportions and ratios right as that is the most important aspect of illustrating or drawing for fashion. Beginner drawing courses can train you to do this, so if you can join a course, good for you. If not, learn by trial and error. In any case, remember to practice.

3. Start a Fashion Journal Pronto

As mentioned earlier, a journal is different from your portfolio; you maintain a journal for yourself. It's a place where you jot down your ideas and anything that inspires you creatively. Start a fashion journal at the earliest even if you do take time to get around working on action plan points 1 and 2.

4. Get Inspired

It is very important for creative people to go beyond their field of interests. For example, iconic film-makers don't just watch films. Woody Allen incorporates philosophy, poetry and classical music into his films and has various interests that inspire him. You may be interested in fashion design but explore other areas of interest and nurture other passions beyond the world of fashion for inspiration and ideas.

2

Your First Business Plan

Double-headed gods are popular in ancient mythology. The Roman culture has Janus, who is supposed to be looking at both the past and the future at the same time. Closer home, the Hindu God Agni is represented by two heads – one a face of kindness while the other the ruthless strength to burn anything to ashes. You're probably wondering what on earth do double-headed Gods have to do with your desire to conquer the world as a hot-shot fashion designer and entrepreneur, but be warned: having two heads is particularly important for an independent fashion designer who aspires to run his or her own business.

Scientists have found that the human brain has two sides that work in tandem. However, most of us are dominated by one of the two sides. In popular psychology, this is often called the Left-brain, Right-brain theory. According to this theory, those dominated by their left brain tend to be analytical, scientific and rational in their approach to problem solving and life. The right-brain thinkers tend to be artists, poets and, you guessed it right – fashion designers!

As a fashion entrepreneur, you will be expected to draw on both sides of your personality. The creative side will help in

16

producing designs, while the left brain will help in thinking about your business rationally. This is essential for long-term success. Keep this image of yourself in mind: a modern-day Fashion Janus, or a new-age creative Fashion Agni with two heads.

In Chapter 1, we discussed putting together your fashion journal, your first portfolio and expanding your scope of inspiration. These are areas that appeal to your creative side. However, for any entrepreneurial endeavour to be deemed a success, it has to start making profits. Here, I offer ideas that I hope will stimulate you and lead to the growth of that second, all important head – the head of an entrepreneur.

I recommend that you start thinking like an entrepreneur or a business person right from the beginning. This means integrating your efforts toward becoming a better designer with learning how to run a business successfully.

EVERY BUSINESS MUST START WITH A BUSINESS PLAN

There are many avenues for those who want to pursue fashion designing as a career. Many work as designers for another's brand, and can focus exclusively on their growth as a designer. But you're different. You aspire to have a fashion label of your own. Setting up a fashion label is like setting up any other business. It is like opening a café, setting up a bookshop or starting your own e-commerce website. And every business has to start with a plan. Never heard of a business plan? Heard of it but don't know what exactly it contains? Have an MBA and feel insulted that I think you don't know what a business plan is?

No matter how well you know or don't know how a business plan works, you will find the following section beneficial.

What Is a Business Plan?

Simply put, it is a plan to chart the future of your business. There are several standards for a good business plan, but at the end of the day there no real rules, just so long as your plan gives you a clear idea of where you see your business going. You can choose to make it as pictorial or creative as you wish. Broadly, a business plan answers the following questions.

1. Where is your fashion design business going?
2. How is your fashion label going to grow at the end of this year?
3. How is it going to grow, year on year?

The business plan will also have to cover other aspects of your business, such as how much your outfits should cost, the market you intend to target, the investments you wish to seek, etc.

Why Is a Business Plan Required?

1. You need a business plan to think through your goals and objectives clearly and rationally.
2. To share the future plan of your business with others, such as investors, lenders, banks, managers, partners, etc.
3. To help you make important decisions. Based on the business plan, you can better identify and prioritize important decisions that need to be made.
4. To help you work on crucial strategic areas such as sales, marketing and expansion.

You will understand all these points better once you have gone through this chapter, and better still when your own business plan has been written. In the following sections, we ask you a series of question under various headers that you will need to answer to do just that. At first you might be uncomfortable. You may not know whether you can fill in your fashion journal, forget your portfolio book. And the last thing you expect to know is where your business is going to go at the end of the year!

Well, that's the magic of the business plan. It forces you to consider all these aspects before diving headlong into a full-fledged career as a fashion design entrepreneur. It might seem boring, but a little extra effort at this stage can give you a good idea of which way your career is headed.

An average business plan has over ten pages and at least over 3,500 words. Don't sweat, we feature 'Explore' links and 'Do it' tips in-between, so you can work on those if you need a break from writing your business plan in one shot. You can also skip to other chapters and keep coming back to this one, to complete your plan bit by bit.

DO IT!

Okay, so you're not a good writer or are just too intimidated to write that much? How about recording your business plan? Most phones these days come with a video/audio record option. So just do it! No excuses. Also, did you know you can write your business plan in any language you choose? Hindi, Kannada or Kashmiri. Absolutely! If ever you need to present your plan to investors or others, simply get it translated for a few hundred bucks.

How to Write Your First Business Plan?

1. Each of the sections that a standard business plan contains is listed below.
2. Beneath each section header are descriptions about that section and a list of questions.
3. Answer the questions under each of the sections and you will be done by the time the chapter ends.

Should You Write Your Business Plan in One Sitting?

Probably not. We suggest doing a couple of sections first and the rest as you continue reading the chapters of this book. As you get more information and perspective about the different areas of your business, you can gradually tackle the other sections. Take at least three weeks to write your first business plan.

I've made it super, super simple for you. Follow the guidelines under each of the section headings and answer the questions for maximum benefit. (Write these down, whether on paper on in a word document on your computer. Keep saving as you write your plan!)

As the first step, title your document. We suggest 'My Business Plan', followed by the name of your brand.

1.0 EXECUTIVE SUMMARY

This section of the business plan will contain a summary of all the information in the subsequent sections. We can come back to this later, but do type this header out on your document as a reminder to fill it in later.

2.0 COMPANY PROFILE

This section is further broken down into eight different sub-sections (the headers with no numbers are sub-sections). This is a crucial section of your business plan, so please pay attention to the points mentioned below.

What Is Your Business About?

1. When was your company established? Or, when is your business going to be registered? Refer to Chapter 3 for more information on this process.
2. What is special or unique about your products?
3. Include any illustrations, ideas or photographs you may have pertaining to your clothes or accessories.

Company History

1. When did you first think of setting up your company?
2. What is the inspiration behind it?
3. If you already have an existing company, write a little about the first product you sold and your journey so far. If you're in the process of setting up a company, you could put in a little story about the idea you intend to follow.

Management

1. For the opening sentence of this section, fill up the blanks: <Company Name>is fully owned and operated by <name/s of the people who own and run your fashion company>.

2. Now, follow this up with your/your partner's bio/s. A bio is a small summary of your educational qualifications, work experience and professional achievements. You can also make your bio creative by including what you wish to achieve, interesting hobbies and interests. For example: 'Sarita is also an avid film buff and has watched all of Felini's films' or 'Vijay also happens to be an avid trekker and has trekked the Mount Kailash!'

Location

1. Where is your business going to be based? Will it be based at home? Will you have an office? Write it down in a sentence and put your business address next to it.
2. Are your designs sold at a store already? If so, write that down. If not, write about where you would like your designs to be sold and how soon you reasonably expect that to happen. Read Chapter 8 for more information about approaching retailers.
3. Do you intend to sell online? Do you intend to sell on Facebook? Or do you have a deal with an e-commerce venture? Chapter 8 has more about selling online, including setting up your own online store.
4. The key information needed for this section is where your primary office or workshop is based and the locations where your clothes are or will be sold.

Legal Structure

Will you run your business as a sole proprietorship? Will you set it up as company? (Read Chapter 3 for more information on this.) However, you will need to consult a chartered account on what structure works best for you. Most independent entrepreneurs run their business as 'sole proprietors'.

Vision and Mission

While this sub-section is not very big, it is very important. It answers two very important questions:
1. Mission: What is my business going to achieve/provide/do/be?
2. Vision: How is my business going to go about doing this?

The sentences you put down now can be your starting point. You may want to keep coming back and tweaking this until your brand is established.

EXPLORE!

Google 'Mission and Vision Statements' of famous fashion companies you admire. For example: Chanel's Mission Statement is 'To be the Ultimate House of Luxury, defining style and creating desire, now and forever.' Can you find mission or vision statements for top five fashion houses?

Goal and Objectives

1. This will be unique and personal to your business.
2. Decide your goals. List them out. Try not to have more than three or four goals.
3. Also, do restrict your goals to the first or between the first and third year of your business. For example, if you're a new

designer with a new business your first goal could also be something like this.

Goal 1: Put together your first ever collection for the upcoming Spring-Summer season. Other goal examples include: Have at least one retail tie-up by the end of the year.

Or

Sell at least five outfits on social media within the first three months.

Professional Advisors

Do you intend to or have already hired any expert advisors? Mention this information. (Also refer to Chapter 3 where we cover employee-related issues.)

Congratulations! You have just completed 10% of your business plan.

3.0 MARKET RESEARCH

You should ideally work on this section after doing some research on other businesses in your industry. I have a simple suggestion: complete the following section in two to three sittings. In the first and second sitting, research the questions listed in the next section, and in the third, put it all together neatly in a business plan-style. Many of the questions listed in the following section have suggestions on how to find the relevant answers you need.

Industry Profile and Outlook

This section tests your knowledge about your industry. Answer it as though you were writing an essay on 'The Fashion

Industry in India'. Answer these questions to complete your essay.

1. What is the current state of the fashion industry in India? Look for articles on the industry in leading business newspapers and magazines like *Business Today*, *Economic Times*, *Hindustan Times*, *Mint*, etc. Based on your research, answer this question accurately.

EXPLORE!

Google 'Fashion Industry India' + 'Business Today' or other publications of your choice such as 'HT Mint', 'Economic Times', etc.

---

2. What kinds of clothes/accessories are being designed for men/women/children today? Answer this question with the information most relevant to your business. Are you designing for women? Are you designing accessories? Answer based on the research for question 1.

3. What are consumer attitudes towards your business? News articles or formal/informal surveys help in answering this one. Put together a couple of questions and get friends and family to answer them, and if possible, to distribute the survey to as many of their friends as possible. Ensure that the right target group answers your survey. For instance, if you're making clothes for children between five and ten years old, get a bunch of young mothers to answer your questions.

4. What kinds of retail stores are stocking your kind of products?

5. Are clothes like the ones you're producing being sold online? Where? Note as many details as you can find.

6. Do you understand the psychology or thoughts and emotions behind consumer shopping in your category? Simply put, what would draw people to buying the kind of clothes you design? Think about it a bit and jot your thoughts down. If you design bridal wear, put yourself in the bride's shoes and imagine the thoughts and feelings that drive her to purchase a particular outfit. If you design gym clothes, what are people looking for: comfort or confidence?

Local Market

If you're a new, young designer, you're obviously looking at starting off with your local market first. Try and answer questions similar to the ones just discussed but with your local market in mind. Since it's probably an area you grew up in or are familiar with, you're at a huge advantage here. It is likely you know what your target audience is looking for or you know enough people to meet and interview for your research.

Target Market

What is your target demographic? Women, men or children? What is the age group? What is their income bracket? Make a list of relevant details. Close your eyes and visualize the person who will buy your clothes. List as many relevant qualities as you can about this person's group from a business perspective.

CONGRATULATIONS! YOU'VE COMPLETED 50 PER CENT OF YOUR BUSINESS PLAN!

4.0 SALES & MARKETING

Pricing Strategy

Pricing can be tricky for a new entrepreneur. Being too expensive risks losing customers who don't want to invest heavily in a new designer. Pricing too low, however, may be financially unviable. Chapter 6 of this book deals extensively with how to figure out pricing strategies. Read up and work on building a solid, well-thought-out strategy. Generally speaking, this section should include how much you intend to charge for your clothing or accessories and why.

Marketing Strategy

Once again, your marketing strategy has to be well thought-out. Chapter 5 of this book deals extensively with that topic. Refer to it for ideas on how to build your brand. Remember that you will need a detailed plan of how you intend to market your products.

Do you intend to set up a social media page? Will you have a blog? Will you hire a PR agency to try and feature your work in magazines? Will you try and enter a prominent fashion week? Marketing costs money and none of these suggestions are cheap, except for social media and blogging. You will have to balance your budget while spreading the word about your brand.

Sales Strategy

How will you sell your products? Chapter 8 of this book has a few ideas to get you started on retailing your products. This is the hardest but the most important part of your business plan.

Remember, you're not doing this to present to an investor. This is the first-ever business plan you will be making and you will do it for yourself. It doesn't have to be perfect.

DO IT!

Do you have a family member you look up to? Or a friend with an MBA degree? You can get them to help you try and understand each of the components of Section 4.0 – Marketing Strategy, Pricing Strategy and Sales Strategy. It is important for you to understand the relevance of these sections, independent of the fashion industry.

EXPLORE!

The pricing, sales and marketing strategies of famous brands are online, with analyses by many experts. Here's an example for you to start the process of exploration: Google: 'Marketing Strategy' + 'Zara' or 'Pricing Strategy' + 'Chanel' or 'Sales Strategy' + 'H&M'. Feel free to interchange any of the phrases and brand names and see what pops up. Try adding 'India' to see if there's specific information that could help you. But do remember, copying the pricing, marketing or any other strategy found on the Internet for your business plan isn't going to help. Besides, you're smarter than that.

5.0 ADMINISTRATION

Location

1. Which city will you operate from?
2. What is the address of your home office or boutique/primary retailer?
3. Do you have a website?

Legal

Have you registered your brand name? (Chapter 3 will tell you how to do this). If you have been through the process already, mention the registered brand name here fully.

Human Resources

List the number of your employees, including full-time and part-time employees (and consultants as well). If you intend to hire employees over the course of the next six months or year, do mention it.

Process

Here, in about ten steps, explain the process of how you will produce your clothes, accessories or jewellery. Also, include a sample selling strategy. Complete the entire cycle from ideation to sale. For example:

Step 1: Will produce sketches of five designs with the master tailor at the beginning of the week.

Step 2: Tailor will be hired to work four hours a day and will produce at least three of the five designs by the end of the week. Designer will meet with the tailor every day to discuss design and progress.

Step 3: Designer will create the labels to be sewn onto the clothing from their home-office boutique.

Step 4: Professional photographer known to the designer and working at a reduced rate will photograph the completed designs.

Step 5: Completed designs will be emailed to website that designer currently has a tie-up with.

(This is just a sample process break-up and is not to be taken as a complete or accurate process cycle. Work out your own planned process and include it in this format.)

Risk Assessment

This section is one of the major reasons why start-up designers should make a business plan. If you're proceeding in a detailed manner, by this point you should have noticed that some decisions need backup plans to cover different eventualities. In this section, you basically have to explain what you will do if Plan A doesn't work; how you will move to Plan B, or even to Plan C. The questions below will help you think about this section in a more concrete way.

What are the major risks facing your business today? For a small start-up business in this industry, risks could be anything from having only one master tailor who quits abruptly in the middle of work, to running out of your initial investment before making any profits.

1. Make a list of risks. Do you have strategies to offset each of these risks? Note the strategy down next to the corresponding risk.
2. Consider also what to do if your initial plans and strategies to overcome the risks don't work out.

CONGRATULATIONS! YOU'VE COMPLETED 80 PER CENT OF YOUR BUSINESS PLAN!

6.0 FINANCIALS

Start-up Costs

Calculate as accurately as possible how much money you will need to get your business up and running. Write that down here. For instance, your start-up cost could include the total amount it would take to get your first twenty creations out into the market. You could further elaborate on this aspect by listing them this way.

1. Start-up costs: Registration, etc.
2. Start-up assets: Your savings, materials and equipment that you may have already invested in, such as fabrics, sewing machines, etc.
3. Start-up financing: The loan you are taking or the investors involved (even if that happens to be your family, it will be good idea to put that down in writing here).

Chapter 7 of this book also explores the various funding options available to a fashion entrepreneur.

Break-even Analysis

A. Business Cost: How much will it cost to run your business for a fixed period? This can be between six months and a year. Calculate everything, including manufacturing costs, utilities, your own living expenses, salaries, etc. The more logical and realistic you can be about this figure, the better for you!

Please note that manufacturing costs include everything – buying material, accessories, tailoring, etc. Make a separate note of this, as you will need it later.

B. Sale Price: What is your total estimated sale price? (The total amount of all the goods you hope to sell.)

C. Manufacturing Cost: What is your total estimated manufacturing cost? (This is the total amount it will cost to produce your products. This will need to be calculated from the 'business costs' above.)

Subtract your estimated sale price (B) with your manufacturing price (C). Now, divide the result by the total cost to run your business (A).The result you get is the number of pieces of merchandise – clothing or accessories or jewellery – that you have to sell to break even. For example, if your result is 100, this means you have sell 100 pieces of clothing to run your business without making any profit ('at cost').

The break-even point is important, because though you wouldn't have made a profit by this point, you wouldn't have made a loss either. This is the point where you get back exactly what you put in, financially speaking, and you know that your business can, at the very least, stay afloat.

Sales Forecast

Here, it is important to think more with the head than with the heart. Not only is it important to think logically, but also intelligently. For instance, a logical assessment may lead you to anticipate low to very low sales in the first three or even six months. An intelligent assessment above that may find key periods when your target market happens to shop more. If you're targeting young adults, your products may be in demand during the beginning of the college term. Try and break your sales forecast into a monthly assessment for about a year or so.

CONGRATULATIONS! YOU'VE COMPLETED 95 PER CENT OF YOUR BUSINESS PLAN.

The End

Dear reader, aspiring fashion designer and entrepreneur, you have now almost completed your first business plan! Remember the first section titled 'Executive Summary'? Now, go back to it and write a small summary of your entire business plan in about 300 or 400 words. Then you will be truly done.

EXPLORE!

Have you ever seen TV shows that are centred on wannabe entrepreneurs presenting their business plans to venture capitalists? No? Well there are tons of international (mostly American shows) of this nature. For example, the hugely popular *Shark Tank*. Go ahead,

Google it. CNBC TV 18 in India has been running a show called *Start-up Indian Funding Challenge*, in which entrepreneurs present their ideas. Run search 'Start-up Indian Funding Challenge' on www.youtube.co.in. This will help you understand better how business plans are presented and evaluated.

DO IT!

After catching a couple of videos or TV shows where entrepreneurs present their ideas to venture capitalists, invite a friend or a family member with experience of running a business and present your business plan. This mock presentation will get you an informed perspective and will make you feel more objective about your business plan. You will find points you feel strongly about and understand areas that you felt didn't sound convincing. Try it. You'll have fun!

3

HIRING, FILING TAXES AND REGISTERING YOUR LABEL

After graduating from the National Institute of Fashion Technology in Mumbai, Tanya Sharma went on to create her own label, 'Gaga'. When asked why she chose not to take up a job first, she said, 'I wanted to be my own boss. I just couldn't imagine working for someone else. Maybe it's just me, but that's the reason why I started my own business.' Many strong individuals are driven to entrepreneurship for the same reason. In some ways, it's a moment of triumph to hire an employee. Knowing that your entrepreneurial efforts are not just making you successful but also contributing to another person's income can be quite rewarding.

But, as the saying goes, be careful what you wish for. 'Dealing with labour in India as an entrepreneur with a small business is one of the most difficult aspects of the job,' says designer Sohni Makkar. Poverty, lack of organized skill training and a lack of education can come with a unique set of challenges, especially in the designer's workshop or studio. 'Petty workshop squabbles are not uncommon,' she adds. But patience and perseverance have paid off for Sohni. 'My children have been educated from your business,' Sohni's master tailor once told her. He was her very first employee.

BE YOUR OWN HANDYMAN OR WOMAN

It's hard to reconcile couturier JJ Valaya's larger-than-life image with his description of his first studio. 'My father was working and living in Delhi when I decided to launch my own label. Fortunately for me, this meant I had access to his 1,100 sq. feet apartment in Delhi. There were two bedrooms, one for me and the other for my dad. The dining room was converted to a studio, where one master tailor, another tailor and one embroiderer would work. I would meet my customers in the drawing room,' he recalls. Today, his workshop in Delhi employs hundreds of karigars, tailors and administrators, and his name Valaya (which was shortened from Ahluwalia), is the epitome of luxury ethnic couture.

Most designer-entrepreneurs have begun with one or two employees, and the designer invariably takes on many roles. As JJ Valaya says, 'I was the handyman. Even if a needle broke, I would run to the market to get it.'

'Until recently, I handed out salaries myself,' says Sohni. Now, having hired a chartered account, she quips: 'I wish I had done it sooner.' On the other hand, twenty-four-year-old upcoming designer Sekuzo travels himself to source fabrics for his collection, making trips to Guwahati, Kolkata, Shillong and even Delhi.

But there's only so much you can do by yourself. Slowly, you must start hiring more people, delegate responsibilities and build a brand that grows not just through your efforts but also through the contribution of your employees.

For several years Kolkata-based award-winning jewellery designer Eina Ahluwalia ran most of her business herself until her sister Atikaa Ahluwalia joined her as the brand head. 'Atikaa has a Masters in Fashion Merchandising from NIFT Delhi, and has worked with Madura Garments as a part of the start-up team for "The Collective" (a premium lifestyle retail chain). So for her to join me was great. It was the perfect combination of having someone who is the right fit professionally, along with the trust and comfort of working with family. She takes care of marketing, distribution, PR, as well as new initiatives in taking the brand forward. Not only was it impossible to try and do all of this along with design and production myself, but also as personalities, we are perfectly aligned to our spheres of work. Even though I've been making jewellery since 2003, it's only once Atikaa joined us in 2009 that we've been able to make an impact on the national and international market in a big way,' says Eina.

WHAT DOES A TEAM AT A BIG FASHION LABEL LOOK LIKE?

Before I offer you a list of tips and suggestions on hiring the right people for a fashion start-up, here's a brief list of employees that a mid-sized fashion design agency could consider employing. Knowing the kind of technical expertise available in the fashion industry, this can help inspire you to grow your label and build a business where most portfolios have been delegated to specialists. This way you will have enough time to focus on the aspects you yourself consider important. Sound good? Okay, here we go.

Design Assistants

Most established labels have at least a couple of design assistants helping out the design head. The posts of design assistants are typically filled by fashion institute graduates, who take up a plethora of tasks from helping the designer prepare for an upcoming fashion show, to finding fabrics, to developing patterns.

Mumbai-based designer Tanya Sharma, whose three-year-old label Gaga Studio was shortlisted for the Vogue Fashion Fund in 2013, describes the role of assistants in the fashion industry. 'Assistants have to be incredibly hard-working because a lot is expected of them at a label. They have to treat the label as if it's their own. Unless they're passionate about the head designer's vision, they won't be able to give their hundred per cent. I have never shirked responsibility or refused to carry out any tasks and I expect the same level of commitment from my assistant,' she says.

Merchandiser

The merchandiser has in-depth market knowledge, a knack for numbers, and coordinates with different teams like sales and manufacturing to optimize the label's development. A merchandiser is expected to provide inputs on market trends, inventory, product categories and will have a direct impact on the label's sales.

Sourcing Managers

As the name suggests, sourcing managers are responsible for sourcing a range of resources from fabrics to embellishments to accessories. The sourcing team also ensures that the best possible raw material is procured at the lowest possible rate. Thus, a good sourcing team contributes to keeping manufacturing costs low. As a designer with a new start-up label and no funds to hire a sourcing manager, you may want to cultivate a 'sourcing manager' mentality. Don't give in to impulse buys that your creative side demands. Aim to keep the quality of your material high while keeping costs low.

Chartered Accountants

While it may be hard to imagine an accounts team in a swanky Dolce & Gabbana office, chartered accountants are often incredibly crucial to the business (which is also why their services do not come cheap). Your label will need a CA, sooner rather than later to ensure that finances and taxes are in perfect order and don't reflect the chaos of a designer's studio!

Marketing

The importance of marketing in the fashion industry can hardly be overstated. Understanding consumers' desires, communicating them effectively to the label's designers and keeping track of marketing efforts and sales results – with such crucial duties, the marketing team at any top label have their job cut out for them.

Public Relations

Have you wondered how a select few labels get themselves routinely featured in Indian fashion magazines? No doubt, many of them are producing genuinely good work. But for a few that are not yet top-notch, public relations play a crucial role in enhancing visibility. Having a public relations team is an asset and is fast becoming a necessity for growing designers. Upcoming designers, with a budget to spare, may consider hiring an independent or freelance PR professional. With a growing number of fashion designers in the country, talent may no longer be enough to get spotted. Media coverage helps with sales and making the cut at top fashion weeks.

Sales Team

Sales teams play a crucial role in the growth of a fashion label. They work at different levels within the label, and across regions. Entry-level sales staff may be deployed at flagship stores to help customers who walk in. More highly trained and qualified sales staff are usually tasked with approaching retailers and buyers to get the label stocked at high-end retail outlets (read more about retailing in Chapter 8). Senior sales members may work in the main offices, focusing on pricing, strategy and targets, and working closely with marketing teams to grow the brand. Sales teams also include members of the online sales and customer support.

Manufacturing

You're probably imagining a sprawling workshop with expert tailors, embroiders, weavers and other experts bringing your design dreams to reality. But it will be a while before that happens for you. It takes lakhs of rupees to run a full-fledged workshop and most young designers just starting out will probably not be able to afford it. Outsourcing your manufacturing process is the way to go these days and many big, famous designers began their careers by outsourcing production.

Designer Sohni Makkar also suggests fine-tuning one's ability to manage before expanding the team. 'If you're a young woman or man just out of college it may be hard to cope with the demands of people management. It can be quite challenging and I'd suggest to slowly build your skills in the area and expand at a reasonable pace.' (Chapter 6 of this book has more information on the manufacturing process.)

This list is by no means exhaustive. But if you have no real exposure to the inner workings of the fashion industry and have been focusing solely on the creative aspects, the section above should have offered you a glimpse of the world beyond the glamour.

Most designers we spoke to for this book started with an expert tailor who did most things for them in the beginning. Few outsourced their manufacturing needs but did almost everything else on their own. Whether or not you should hire someone for a particular role will depend entirely on how badly you need help and also your ability to pay salaries. 'I hired my first assistant when I had my first show at Lakme Fashion Week,' says designer Tanya Sharma. Although she was showcasing her collection as a new designer, without an assistant she couldn't have coped with the demands of her first fashion show.

HIRING ON A BUDGET: SOME SNEAKY IDEAS

Family Expertise

Can you ask qualified family members for help in their area of expertise, such as manufacturing or accounts? Does your sister have an MBA in marketing? Can she devote some time during the weekends for work on your label? Or a resourceful friend who can work part-time? Think about all the people who can help get your business off the ground. But do remember to get people you can trust. The last thing you need is busy family members and unreliable friends bailing out when you need them the most.

Bang for Buck

Entrepreneurship is lonely and young people may be tempted to take on friends they can hang out with. Remember that if you're already tight on budget, you will want to get a bang for every buck. Hire people who you think can actually contribute to your business and offer a diverse set of skills and talents.

If you think you have something to offer interns, such as training, exposure and a productive use of their time (not just free labour for you!), go right ahead and get them on board.

Hiring part-time employees can also help a young business find its feet for less. While some independent consultants can charge a hefty fee, if you are confident of a certain specialist and your business can benefit from her expertise, consider it an investment.

DEALING WITH THE LAW

Indian tax systems, labour laws and other regulations are not simple to deal with. I highly recommend that entrepreneurs consult a chartered accountant and a lawyer at appropriate times and ensure their business complies with all government rules and policies.

Here are some tricky areas that you should be aware of as a fashion entrepreneur.

Business Structure

At some point, you will have to choose a legal structure for your business. Many entrepreneurs choose to be 'sole proprietors' or enter into 'limited liability partnerships'. Depending on the kind of structure you choose for your fashion label, you will have to follow a set of specific rules and be aware of the risks and advantages attached to the particular legal structure. Get informed about all your options and consult a lawyer and a chartered accountant before making your decision. These consultations are not as expensive as you think and rates are often negotiable, especially if you hire an independent professional.

Tax Issues

Depending on where you run your business and sell your clothes or accessories, you will have to pay both central government and state taxes (CST, VAT, etc). Also, new businesses (start-ups) are eligible for tax exemptions under the Income Tax Act (1961). This could lead to thousands of rupees in savings for your business. Other exemptions include expenses of running the business. However, for any exemptions to kick in, you must maintain proper records. Meet with a CA as soon as you have started your business, and make a list of receipts that you must keep to secure these exemptions. Also, your tax status will depend on the legal business structure you choose (check the previous section).

Labour, Contract and Other Laws

The employees you legally hire and the contracts you sign with vendors, suppliers and consultants must be vetted by a lawyer. Most labour laws protect the worker or the employee. Rarely are entrepreneurs able to comply with each and every regulation. Be sure to discuss with a professional how these and other laws impact your business.

Formalities

As a fashion designer, your career and success will be driven by your creativity and, by extension, your intellect. Isn't it interesting to know that creations born from your intellect are legally protected under Indian law?

Intellectual Property law

Intellectual Property laws (IP laws) have evolved over the last century as the global economy has moved from an industrial world to a knowledge-based one. This means, increasingly, the human workforce is not paid for producing physical products but intellect and knowledge-based ideas. Many fashion designers have used IP laws to protect their designs from infringement in India. However, even established designers fail to take advantage of this law and protect or enhance their intellectual assets.

The most obvious function of IP laws is to protect designs and 'idea-based' property. More importantly, they can be used to sue unethical designers who copy your work. However, they also help enhance the value your business. A business that's driven by creativity, innovation and the intellect can be valued based on not just its physical assets but also intellectual assets.

Evaluating a business for its assets and how much it is worth is called business valuation. Business valuation is essential for various reasons. Some of them are:

1. You may wish, at some point in the future, to sell the business. You must know how much your business is actually worth.
2. You're taking on a new partner. How much do they owe you for a partnership?
3. You need a loan. You will need to approach a lender with an accurate valuation of your business.

The following example will give you a rough idea of how IP laws can enhance the value of your business assets.

Assuming an expert has taken into account your profits, assets, processes and history and valued your business at Rs 25,00,000. If you genuinely feel that your designs have a lot of potential and that they could become classics, or could lead to spin-off designs, merchandising deals and so on, you must get your designs legally registered and make them a part of the valuation process. The fact that your designs are registered and an intellectual property audit has been done means the value of your business can also double. After taking into consideration your registered designs and their financial potential, your business could go from being valued at Rs 25,00,000 to Rs 50,00,000 instead.

As soon as you begin to gain recognition and maturity as a label, you may want to consider consulting a lawyer about registering your designs under IP laws. Now that you understand what intellectual property means, here are a few common legal words in the industry (that everybody uses but doesn't necessarily understand!)

Copyrights

Fashion designers can register their work under the Indian Copyright Act (1957), which offers protection against infringement. Design sketches are typically registered under this copyright law and the protection kicks in as soon as the designs have been produced in tangible form.

Trademarks

Designers trademark their logo, brand name and other symbols or patterns that they've come up with. This is important because as your brand takes off, counterfeit designs may appear in the market using patterns or symbols close to your logo or patterns. By trademarking essential elements, you can protect your brand value. Trademarks are covered under Indian Trademarks Act (1999).

Patents

If you believe that you've invented something new with your design, then you can go ahead and patent it. For instance, the wrap dress was first designed by Diane von Furstenberg. She secured her design with a patent and nobody could claim to have 'invented' the wrap dress except Diane. Patents can also extend to fabrics. Patents are covered under the Indian Patents (Amendment) Act, 2000.

Design Act

The Design Act (2000) offers the most protection to fashion designers. The law caters to all the visual aspects of the design that you may create, such as pattern, silhouettes, colours, etc. In essence, all the visual elements that makes your design unique. Registering your design under the Design Act gives you the exclusive right to use that design.

HOW TO REGISTER YOUR BRAND NAME?

In other words, how does one get that R-in-a-circle symbol next to your logo? In India, brand names are registered under the Trademarks Act. Most designers hire lawyers to do this for them. However, knowing what registration of a brand name entails is only helpful. We'll show you how simple it is and just in case you've been putting it off, you'll get on the job right away!

The five simple steps that lead to brand name registration:

Step 1: Deciding the Name

You will start by finding a unique name for your fashion business. As far as possible, try and ensure that the name you've decided upon is not being used by another business in the fashion industry. Many designers simply pick their first name. Sabyasachi Mukherjee calls his label 'Sabyasachi' and Jagsharan Jit Singh Ahluwalia became 'JJ Valaya'.

Step 2: The TM1

After you've found a name you have to complete and submit the TM1 form. The TM1 form can be found on www.ipindiaonline.gov.in. The website also provides links for filing trademark applications online.

Step 3: Supporting Documents

Along with the TM1 form, you will have to include a few supporting documents. (Check with your CA or lawyer.)

Step 4: Filing Paperwork

You can file the TM1 at the Registrar of Trade Marks in your city (if there is one) or just file it online on www.ipindiaonline.gov.in

Step 5: Your 'TM'

Before your brand name is registered, it is scrutinized by the relevant department at the Registrar; typically, it will be about three months before you know if your brand name has been accepted for registration. Once your application is accepted and your brand name and logo have been registered, you will receive a certificate that officially states that your label is protected by law. Now you can use that little R in a circle ®next to your logo!

Just in case you're wondering about the difference between ™ and ®, let's clear that up. Although the™ symbol looks official, it does not mean the brand name or logo is registered. It simply means that you are using it as a claim of uniqueness. If you wish to legally protect your brand name, you should get it 'trademarked' or registered and use the ® sign.

INSPIRATION — TANYA SHARMA

Tanya, a graduate of the National Institute of Fashion Technology in Mumbai (2009) launched her own label.

Gaga is showcased at the Lakme India Fashion Week every year and has also been shortlisted for the Vogue India Fashion Fund in 2013. A Mumbai-based label, Gaga is sported by a host of celebrities including Bollywood stars and famous fashionistas like Sonam Kapoor and Deepika Padukone. This simple girl from Chandigarh, as Tanya likes to describe herself, has definitely made it in B-town!

'Gaga is my nickname. It has been since the day I was born! I have always been called 'Gaga'. When I was thinking about branding my label, I thought going with Gaga was a good idea. It is short, unique and meant 'going crazy about something' – an idea I really liked. Which designer wouldn't like people going gaga over their designs? So I felt it had a happy vibe, which is something I want my designs to have as well. And Gaga it was going to be.

'As far as registering my brand name is concerned, it was so much easier than I expected. Thankfully, in India, most basic legal services are relatively cheap and so I got it done through a lawyer in no time. I would recommend this to other young designers as well. I worked with a law firm that specializes in getting label and company registrations. It is a very easy process and you have to fill a form and submit some documents.

'The first time you see your registered brand name and logo, it is like seeing your baby brought to life. As someone once said, when you create something – and it can be anything – a piece of art, a flavourful dish, your brand logo ... it's like putting a part of you out there. It gives you a sense of great pride.

'Just when my brand started taking off, Lady Gaga became this huge international celebrity. But you know what? I will stick to my label name because that's me. That's who I grew up as – Gaga.'

2-POINT ACTION PLAN

1. Temporary Assistantship

If you're thinking about being an entrepreneur, apply for a temporary assistantship with an upcoming fashion designer. Choose a designer who is a few steps ahead of you. Perhaps, you already have a small business from home, in which case you can reach out to a designer with a studio and a few employees. Remember that you may or may not get paid for this gig. Do it to observe and learn how the designer deals with her employees, copes with the financial pressures of a small business, and more. If you intend to do this for a short while, make sure you've made your intentions clear to your employer.

2. Trademark Inspiration

Call a lawyer's office and find out how you can register your company name. Take notes. Keep these notes in a place where you can refer to them, or add to them as inspiration strikes, as often as possible.

4

DESIGN

The fashion industry recruits a range of experts from market gurus to data managers and engineers to chartered accountants. The scale of your business and the number of expert hands you have on board will determine the complexity of design and manufacturing that your business can sustain. For instance, if you're starting with a single tailor, you may find that your process is simple with no mood-boarding, pattern-making, draping, etc. 'When you start with one expert tailor, like I did, he's your cutter, pattern-maker, technical designer,' says Chandigarh-based designer Sohni Makkar.

Even if the design process seems daunting, it isn't. You can start small and pick up skills as you grow your business or take up assistantships and part-time jobs to learn the ropes.

FROM CORPORATE CORRIDOR TO GOLD DUST

When management graduate-turned-designer Eina Ahluwalia decided to take up jewellery design, even her staunchest supporters tried to dissuade her, telling her that the industry was too niche, complicated and difficult. Nonetheless, she quit her job in the early 2000s to explore the possibility of making interesting hand-crafted silver jewellery. Eina found that investing the time to understand the design and production process paid off. 'With jewellery, you create something of value. It has permanence,' she says. Indeed, many of Eina's classic pieces, launched during different fashion seasons, continue to be in demand. For instance, her haathphool (hand adornment piece), launched as part of the Wedding Vows collection in 2011, is in vogue even now.

While you may not know everything you need to about the technical aspects of fashion designing, you should grab every opportunity that comes your way to add to your skills. Others in Eina's position may have chosen to invest in a course on jewellery designing, but, Eina started off experimenting on her own. When her business took off in a few years, she invested the time and resources in apprenticeships abroad. 'It was a kind of re-investment into my business,' she says.

THE DESIGN PROCESS, UNPACKED

If you are not a trained designer, you may be intimidated when you come across the various processes involved in professional design and production. Here, I unpack the design cycle by breaking down some of the steps typically involved in getting a collection out. As I mentioned earlier, this is not a training manual for design, but instead it takes you through the basics in the hope that you will use it as a foundation to learn more. Don't treat the following list as complete or exhaustive, but as an outline that you can fill in with content as your career takes off. The steps are not numbered because they can be interchanged during the design process. However, a basic chronological structure has been maintained.

Concept Board

In Chapter 1, I introduced you to the idea of having your own fashion journal. The journal is different from a designer's portfolio for a collection. The fashion journal is a collage of all the elements that have inspired you to create a collection that can be found in your portfolio. A fashion journal is also something you keep for a longer period of time. It's a book you reach for when you need inspiration.

The concept board, also known as a mood board or theme board, closely correlates to a collection. This is not a random collage of inspirations, it serves a specific purpose. After deciding on the theme for your collection, you seek inspiration in various places and go about creating your concept board.

For instance, say you want to launch an Indian summer collection based on the Mughal period. You can have visuals from the hit Hindi film *Jodha Akbar* based on that period. You can have the famous Mughal-era paintings with their classic side-angle figures. You can have poetry or ghazals from the period. You can also include practical elements like visuals of your target audience – a picture of a pretty, young, affluent urban girl from the newspapers. Fabric swatches and a couple of colour combinations or patterns can also feature in there. Basically, the concept board should be filled with photographs, illustrations, art, or text (but not too many words) that pertain to your theme. As you design your collection, the concept board remains as a reference point. It is a source of inspiration and direction – you set boundaries based on the concept board, or let it liberate you creatively.

DO IT!

Think of a theme for a collection. Don't worry about having the perfect theme. It can be absolutely anything. Create a concept board for it, based on the example and explanation given earlier.

EXPLORE!

Go to www.pinterest.com and, in the search box on the home page, key in: 'creative mood boards fashion'. You will find lots of inspiration on concept boards.

Research

Did you know that designers take anywhere between a year and two years to design their collection? The design process is preceded by research. Research is crucial in any professional fashion design set-up. The information you collect from your research will give you the foundation to create rich, original and unique designs. After all, even the most creative people need something concrete to base their ideas on.

For instance, in the previous point, I gave you an example of a summer design collection based on the Mughal period. You surely can't just stop by watching the film *Jodha Akbar*! Your research will have to be deeper for better ideas. If you have a good local bookshop or library that stocks historical books, perhaps you can start by bringing a few home. Thanks to the

Internet, you can always order books online. Further, you can look up hundreds of paintings from the period on the Internet. You might also want to find poetry from famous poets of the time to see if you can find descriptions of clothes or to get a sense of aesthetics.

Further, you will have to spend a fair bit of time researching market trends, fabrics and colours that are in vogue. Irrespective of the theme of the collection, your designs will have to be based on current market trends.

Brainstorming

After research, brainstorming is one of the most crucial steps in the creative process. This process is so important that at large fashion houses, members of the design team can often be found sitting together and brainstorming on various aspects of the design, the theme and more. As an independent designer, while you create your concept board and research your theme, you will have to keep building on your idea by brainstorming.

Often, the first idea that we come up with is the most obvious one. Brainstorming helps minimize the risk of being stuck with the most obvious idea. It is typically done in a group, but you can also apply the same techniques while working on an idea by yourself. While working alone or in groups, a common brainstorming technique used is called mind-mapping. It involves creating a flowchart style text-and-visual 'map' of your ideas or thought process.

If you've never heard of brainstorming or mind-mapping, don't worry. It is not at all complicated and not half as boring as it sounds. In all likelihood, you've probably done it but just don't know what it's called. As a creative person, you may find these tools really useful.

EXPLORE!

Log onto Amazon.co.in or a similar online store featuring books, and search for books on brainstorming. Read free previews of as many books that interest you on the subject. You may find fun brainstorming activities, exercises and more. Obviously, if you find any of the books interesting, get them!

DO IT!

Visual stimulation time. Use the Google images tool (go to google.co.in and click the 'images' link). Type in 'mind-mapping fashion design'. Find samples of mind maps. Based on what you find, try and create your own mind map of an idea or theme you've been thinking about for a fashion line.

Sketching

Many designers like to sketch and illustrate their designs before moving on to the next step. For those who like to visualize the design almost a 100 per cent in their mind before doing anything else, this becomes a crucial step. However, many designers go back to their sketches along the way. They may make little tweaks to their designs based on factors like fabrics or colour combinations or simply because they changed their mind. However, professional designers are always pressed for time and often can't keep making changes after their production process has begun.

Many designers also rely on their assistants, or even specialist illustrators, to make the sketches for them. Young designers who are just starting out, especially those not very experienced in their drawing or fashion illustration skills, may spend minimal time on this step. As long as your tailors and other workers involved in the manufacturing process have a clear idea of your design, it should be fine.

Sourcing or Creating Fabrics and Embellishments

Once the designs and concepts for the collection are in place, the sourcing team at a fashion label begins the process of finding and purchasing the best fabrics, embellishments and accessories required for the design. Internationally, especially in developed countries where labour can be expensive, there are specialized studios that create exciting textiles and fabrics and cater exclusively to designers. In India, many designers prefer to create their own fabrics thanks to the pool of experienced textile workers in this country.

Mumbai-based fashion designer and entrepreneur Tanya Sharma says, 'If you have the opportunity to create your own fabrics, do it! What's the point of just getting pretty looking fabrics from here and there and putting them together? Personally, for me, part of the pleasure of being a fashion designer is creating my own fabrics. If a start-up designer has the resources and the funding, they can invest in creating their own fabrics.'

This is not easy and many designers choose to instead source their material from various vendors. However, Tanya says, 'My suggestion to young designers is to understand fabrics and textiles as well as they can. Perhaps do a course, or even better, travel to small villages and towns that are creative textile hubs. One could go to Kutch in Gujarat and explore the talented array of weaves, textures and designs.'

EXPLORE!

Almost every state in India has its traditional handloom and textiles. Use the Internet to make a list of traditional textiles and handlooms. Aim to put together a list of at least twenty. Google terms: <Name of the state> + Textile + Handloom. Name of the state can be Karnataka, Kerala, Himachal Pradesh, etc.

DO IT!

A swatch book is a collection of swatches or fabric samples. Can you create one of the list of textiles that you've made? You can source these when you travel or when handloom exhibitions come to your city. You can request friends and relatives to send you these textiles. Find a way to get as many fabric samples as you can. Designer Tanya Sharma suggests that young designers do a course in textiles. These activities are as close as you can get to expanding your knowledge bank on textiles and fabrics while running your fashion business!

Finalizing Your Range

As a designer, especially someone who is starting out, every new design can feel special and important. However, most seasoned designers learn to become ruthless in choosing their final range. They may have 500 ideas and over 200 sketches but ultimately make only about 100 outfits for a particular line.

Chennai-based designer and stylist Chaitanya Rao says, 'You just have to make a choice. Be objective about what is truly innovative and special. Besides, you may also have to be aware of what is really trending, what fashion editors have been picking out over the last few seasons, what customers are looking for.' So do your research before whittling down your line to the final few designs, but don't forget to also trust your instincts.

Pattern-making

If you are starting off on a really small budget, like many of the designers interviewed for this book, finding a good master tailor who can also make patterns will be immensely useful. As your business grows, you will be able to afford professional pattern-makers or assistant designers who will do this for you.

If you haven't taken that sewing class yet and are wondering what pattern-making is, don't worry. It's simply a technical term for cutting patterns in paper with specifications. This means, having pieces of your outfits – like the pockets in a dress or the curve of a skirt or a collar – cut out in paper in exact size as the real outfit. The 'patterns' are made out of thick Manila paper. These patterns help tailors cut cloth to perfect specifications, which is an essential step in making that flawless outfit you've designed.

When you work with a master tailor, you will realize they are incredibly good at cutting and need no paper references. So problem solved! (Nonetheless, it helps to know what pattern-making is. And remember, as you get into the fashion business in a big way, pattern-making is going to become an essential part of your professional life.)

EXPLORE!

Go to YouTube.com and search for 'pattern-making classes'. This will lead you to several videos that will actually show you how to make patterns and what a pattern-maker does. From the comfort of your home, you can actually get a sense of attending a session in fashion school. Because pattern-making is such a visual process, you will need the help of videos to understand it better. Watch as many as you can. Enjoy, learn & grow!

DO IT!

This is strictly for novices. Google 'simple free sewing patterns'. You will find hundreds of patterns for various designs. Find one you like and cut out your first pattern in an old newspaper. The next step would be to create a sewing pattern for one of your own designs. Feel ready to do that?

Manufacturing

Manufacturing is the last step in the cycle of production. Designers start off with a concept, make sketches, source fabrics or create their own and eventually, the garments are made. International designers in the developed world and in prime fashion hubs like New York and Paris have been outsourcing their clothes manufacturing to countries like China, Bangladesh, Thailand and India. However, in recent years, industry trade unions and government-backed policies are attempting to revive local manufacturing in even major metros like New York and Los Angeles. On the other hand, thanks to low manufacturing costs, Indian designers execute their designs right here, in India.

As an aspiring fashion entrepreneur, staying abreast of global, national and local manufacturing trends can prove to be very useful. For instance, several months a year, manufacturing houses in India may be less busy. This means that teams of talented, top-notch tailors, who usually cater to international designers and their labels, are relatively free. 'You can always try and work with some of them to execute your designs. This can be cost-effective and one of the few ways a new designer can get small number of pieces done professionally,' says fashion designer and entrepreneur Chaitanya Rao. (Chapter 6 includes more details about the process of manufacturing.)

Distribution and Sales

After the clothes are manufactured, the distribution and sales teams at a fashion label take over. The designers contribute to the marketing and sales efforts by showing their collection at a fashion show. Even at these shows, their sales teams will be hard at work behind the scenes meeting teams from departmental stores, or the managers of big retail chains, or the stylists for celebrities, etc. Distribution essentially entails 'distributing' the clothes to various retail points such as shops, boutiques and warehouses. When it comes to big multinational labels, the distribution process may span half the globe. The designer may design the clothes in New York, the clothes could be manufactured in Vietnam, and the final destination for the finished goods could be stores all over Europe. A label of this scale may also have sales staff working in Asia and Africa as well, getting orders from retail chains for stocks.

GOOD TO KNOW: TECHNICAL DRAWING/ FASHION FLATS

Technical drawings, also known as Fashion Flats, will include all the technical details of the design, including the material being used, proportions, and other components that are essential for the manufacturer. Especially important when the production is outsourced, technical drawings will have the details essential to bring a design to life. As a new designer with a small set-up (such as a single tailor!), you will probably not use technical drawing. However, it is good to know this step involved in professional fashion design and manufacturing. As you scale your business and begin to manufacture in larger numbers, you may hire design assistants who will be able to make fashion flats for your work. Technical drawing as a field has evolved over the years and what used to be done on paper with rulers and pen is now executed with software like CAD (computer-aided design) that enables 2-D and 3-D rendering of images.

The bottom line: aspects like these are good to know of, but not terribly important if you're just starting out from your living room design studio!

INSPIRATION — CHAITANYA RAO

This Chennai-based designer has been in the business since the mid-90s. He's almost entirely self-taught and picked up the essential aspects of design and production through courses, traineeships and employments. Chaitanya was already a seasoned designer when he debuted at Lakme Fashion Week in 2007. Not surprisingly, the show took him from regional success to national prominence.

'After my twelfth standard, I took a short course in cutting and stitching. After this, I toyed with the idea of getting a fashion degree, but there weren't that many good institutes at the time except, maybe, NIFT in Delhi, where there would be thousands of applications for a hundred-odd seats. I used to also sketch very well and felt that I did a better job than what some of the institutes were teaching at the time!

'Finally, I decided to just do an economics degree instead because evening classes were easily available. During the day I worked for a big export and garment manufacturing house, which also has a retail presence today. Everyday, from 8 a.m. to 4 p.m., I would be in the factory and after that I would rush to college and take classes till about 7 p.m.'

'After two years at the company I was working at, I began interacting with the founders of a designer store in Chennai. They were visiting our studio as we had supplied them with some outfits, and saw me sketching. They asked me to do a few designs for them. That's when I began work on my first actual fashion line. I teamed up with another designer and hired a master tailor to work with us. My first collection had a grand total of eight outfits! It was not easy given my full-time work at the manufacturing house and college, but I did it.

'It was my first time so I had to work with whatever I had. I invested all the money that I had saved from two years of employment; at the time my salary was about Rs 2000 a month. I had a friend who modelled the outfits, and we did a small, fun shoot. I have never liked synthetics, and the company where I worked used linen most of the time. For my line, I decided to use silk, khadi silk, hand embroidery and so on. It was a Western collection. Of course I made mistakes. At the time you design thinking everyone's a Kate Moss! So I got orders for different sizes and we catered for those orders. It was a great experience and one I'll never forget. I used muted colours and didn't do anything over the top. So looking back, I think the clothes of that first line can still be worn and are classics of sorts!

'For young designers who want to do something, take the initiative. Nobody is going to approach you. Go out there and meet people. After my tailoring course, I walked into this company and asked for work.'

'Try and do the same. Take the initiative to do a course and get a good grounding in cuts, style and finish. You could also approach an export house to help them with their work and perhaps offer to design a line for them. That could become your first line!

'You also need to up your game if you hope to be stocked at top retail stores and markets. Your finished product has to be good. Try and find innovative ways to get that top product. Many young designers are looking at export houses as an option. If you're looking at moving from your home studio to getting more professional products, network like crazy. Ask friends, relatives, family, etc., for contacts with manufacturers, production units, etc., so you can produce smaller volumes at reasonable costs. It may be a great idea before you get into investing in your own workshop or reach a stage where you're able to afford outsourcing for higher volumes.'

4-WEEK ACTION PLAN – WORKING ON YOUR FIRST COLLECTION

Week 1

1. Do your research on a theme for your very first line. Explore options that you're interested in based on what your label is going to be all about.
2. Create a concept board based on your research and the theme of your design.

Week 2

1. Work on a few designs based on your research and theme, anywhere between 1 and 3, depending on how many you think you can realistically design within a week. Keep it simple and easy.
2. Make sketches if you're good at that or simply jot down outlines and ideas in your fashion journal instead.

Week 3

1. Work on creating patterns for your designs.

Week 4

1. Sew one of your designs if you can or get a master tailor to do it for you.

5

MARKETING, BRANDING AND MORE

'We live in the age of rampant consumerism, where the market is cluttered, and branding is aggressive. A scenario has emerged where it is imperative for you to be heard, to stand out, and establish your brand,' says fashion designer Anita Dongre. She should know, for who hasn't heard of AND, the famous pret label that Anita started in the '90s? AND has stood the test of time and only grown in popularity since then.

So how can you stand out in the glut of new designers and brands that come out every day? One word (among a few others, of course): Marketing.

India has evolved from the days when 'marketing' was another word for shopping! Up until the early '90s, we Indians loved to say 'we are going marketing', if we were heading to the market to buy something; today, of course, most of us know what marketing actually means. In simple terms, it is the process that businesses use to promote or publicize their products and services. Typically, marketing involves advertising, communications and events, branding exercises, etc.

As technology and consumers have evolved, the activities that have come under the gamut of marketing have expanded greatly.

Marketing professionals in fashion also have a greater scope to create buzz-worthy campaigns since the industry is associated with everything that's edgy and innovative – whether its heroin-snorting models with the tagline 'Fashion Junkie' for Italian fashion brand Sisley or Benetton's crazy, provocative ads year after year.

EXPLORE!

Google 'top fashion campaigns' and see what shows up.

WHY DO YOU NEED A GOOD MARKETING STRATEGY?

Before you learn all about marketing, here are a few important reasons why it is very important for an upcoming fashion entrepreneur to have a good marketing strategy in place. Having a glossy photo shoot published in a magazine or getting 100 likes for a design on Facebook can be an ego boost, but your marketing strategy should go beyond making you feel good. It should add value to your sales efforts. Often, marketing may also involve doing things you don't necessarily enjoy. You may not like chasing journalists to feature your brand in their articles, but you may have to do it, at least until your label has grown enough to have a dedicated PR person!

Visibility

Your brand has to be visible in the public domain. Without creating a strategic marketing campaign that increases your visibility, you will limit the reach of your brand. Therefore your marketing strategy must have key elements of visibility such as ads, magazine features, interviews and more.

Brand-building

Brands are not built overnight, and they have to be nurtured with a good strategy. By associating your brand with certain elements such as celebrity-laden campaigns and ideas that you choose, you build an identity for your brand and reinforce your brand values in the public's mind.

Valuation

The more respected your brand, the higher your business valuation will be. This will be important when it comes to finding investors and sourcing funds, going public (listing your business on the stock exchange), or even selling your business. Without a brand, your business is only worth as much as it costs to manufacture the clothes. With a brand name that commands respect and recognition, your business is worth that much more.

Expansion

Aggressive marketing of your brand is important for growth. The better known your label is the more opportunities, offers and options will come your way.

BRANDING VS MARKETING

Marketing costs a lot of money. The marketing budgets of big fashion labels can run into crores. This includes models, photo shoots, ad films, other publicity material and the costs of buying media space like hoardings or television spots. But don't worry, I've got you covered. We have a bunch of realistic marketing ideas for new or upcoming fashion entrepreneurs to employ in this chapter. But before I get to that, let's get one thing out of the way – the difference between branding and marketing. In the preceding paragraph, I've alluded to branding as one of the many marketing activities. However, branding is very important on its own as well.

It is important for businesses to know the difference because you have to know from the start what your brand stands for, and that will define your marketing strategy.

Branding

In simple terms, brand is the name of a business. Coco Chanel, Louis Vuitton, JJ Valaya, Sabyasachi are all brand names. (They also happen to be names of people, but that's not important here.) Essentially, a brand is the name of a business. But what sets it apart from just another name is the fact that brands have values attached to them. Let's take a look at some examples:

- Chanel: Feminine, Independent, Exclusive and Timeless
- Louis Vuitton: Premium, Elegant and Creative
- JJ Valaya: Indian, Royal, Opulent and Celebratory

Without their values or brand values, brands would just be names. Without strong brand values, a brand's marketing strategy is at the risk of failing and ultimately, affecting the business.

How can you determine what your brand stands for? It is difficult, but not impossible. Go back to Chapter 2, where we talk about making a business plan. The chapter forces you to ask yourself close to a hundred questions about your business, including who your target audience is, what is the market situation, what does your label stand for and more. This will help you determine the nature of your brand. Needless to say, your brand values will also have to be determined by who you are and what your vision is.

The Right Marketing Strategy

'While design is absolutely critical to generate consumer interest, market demand and loyalty, a good marketing strategy is essential for the brand to build recognition and equity. Designs have to identify potential consumers from a diverse demographic and psychographic mix, and reinvent the label according to consumer preference and changing trends in fashion. A good marketing strategy helps maintain consistent consumer recall and loyalty,' says designer Anita Dongre.

Big fashion houses typically have an army of experts and strategists who work through the year to come up with the right marketing strategy for the brand. You will have only yourself to rely on for the strategy to begin with (And our ten top tips that we've listed below, of course).

The marketing strategy of a new label will be driven by three important factors. Let's call it BAM!

Brand Values – Audience – Money

Brand Values: We've elaborated on this above. Decide what your brand is all about. Is it a youthful, edgy brand? Or a classic, serious label? This will also be defined by what you design. Are you going to be designing maternity wear or Friday casuals?

Audience: Who are you going to be talking to? An important question to answer, as this can impact the tone of your communication and your entire media plan as well.

Money: There's no point including, multimedia advertising campaign in your marketing strategy if you cannot afford an assistant to your master tailor. Enough said.

How are you feeling so far? Are you with me? If you're a young person driven by an innate desire to design and do nothing else, all this management jargon might sound like gibberish to you. But like I said in Chapter 2, as an entrepreneur you will have to use both the left and right sides of your brain to make your business successful. Devising a good marketing strategy and working on your brand values can be rewarding in the long run. If you love this side of the business and feel like this is an extension of your creative designer side, that's a bonus!

TEN TIPS TO MARKET YOUR BRAND

So you're a new business. You've started making clothes, you've got a small set of loyal buyers too, and you're making some money every month – it's not overflowing, but enough to keep you going as a fashion entrepreneur. How can you start marketing your business with a little money and a lot of love?

1. Get a Website

Domain names (i.e. the name of a site like google.com, facebook.com) are really cheap. You can buy one for less than Rs 500 these days. Indian domain providers are particularly reasonable. Companies like GoDaddy.com offer a bouquet of services and products like web hosting, pre-existing themes, and other options for a few hundred rupees every month. Some websites are easy to maintain and update, some need technical support. If you're not happy with the themes that some of these services offer, you can find freelance web developers and content writers at reasonable cost on sites like elance.com.

If a full-fledged website is not ideal for your business but you'd like to start maintaining an online presence, you can have a blog on platforms like wordpress.com and blogger.com. These blogs can be easily converted to websites at a later point. Blogger platforms also offer hundreds of themes that can work for your fledgling business.

There are several advantages to having a nicely designed professional website. Especially if you've started making a small profit and intend to expand your business. Having a website lends credibility to your business. It sets you apart from other small-time vendors who offer tailoring or other such services from their living room. Also, many journalists and reporters find sources on the Internet. Getting visibility in the press adds to your marketing efforts. All in all, whether your business needs a website is no longer a question these days. The question, if any, is when. In Chapter 8 I tell you how you can build your own e-commerce site.

2. Participate in a Fashion Week/Show

These days there are many fashion weeks, from the famous Lakme Fashion and Wills Fashion weeks to the regional-level North East India Fashion Festival and Bangalore Fashion Week. Participating in these events is a great way to showcase your collection to a larger audience and get the publicity you need. But do remember that this can set you back by a few lakh rupees.

Also, once you do a show, there's pressure to keep showing every year. So while the publicity you receive maybe unprecedented, is your business ready to handle the boost that you may receive after participation? Don't just plan for the show. Plan for after the show as well.

Another important point to remember is choosing the right fashion week or festival. Many of the festivals are covered only in local papers and some of them do not even attract enough industry attention. It may be well worth your time to just focus on your business and try a shot at the new designers' category in one of the bigger fashion weeks. Chapter 9 of this book explores fashion weeks in greater detail.

3. Social Media

'Of late, social media has emerged as an important marketing and communications tool, and unlike traditional means of marketing – hoardings, print advertising, direct mailers – not only is social media cost-effective, it's an instantaneous response medium. It helps you connect with your target consumer, not just locally but globally as well. I see a lot of young designers today using social media as a tool to engage with their consumers and even retail through social media,' says designer Anita Dongre.

Even if you can't build a website or have the time to write a blog, the easiest way to maintain digital presence is social media. But remember, just having a Facebook or Pinterest account for your business is not enough. You must have a strategy. Your social media strategy must be an extension of your marketing strategy and your brand values.

EXPLORE!

Check out Anita Dongre's online presence. AND's online marketing team is hard at work ensuring the brand is visible on multiple platforms. Explore the work they do and get inspired. Google: 'Anita Dongre + Facebook or + Instagram'. 'Anita Dongre + Pinterest'. What is Anita's social media strategy? How does it tie in with her brand values and larger marketing strategy?

---

4. Offers, Discounts and Sales

Who doesn't like a good flat 50 per cent off? Does this mean you should sell your products at half the price to get noticed? No, but it does mean that sales and offers are a great marketing ploy. There's no reason, no matter how young your business is, not to create a buzz using this time-tested technique.

If you've followed the top tip No. 3, you will work on building a good social media presence and get as many followers as you can. How about inviting them to a weekly Monday morning sale? Offer the products that you can afford to sell at a slightly lower cost and still make profit. Keep thinking up new ideas to create a buzz with offers, sales, discounts, contests, etc.

As a young designer the costs of your outfits are likely to be less than other established designer-wear. You can work this to your advantage as well by taking the 'designer goods for less' line. Also, if you have a few sample pieces lying around that you have no use for, you could organize simple contests on social media that could create a buzz for your brand and give away something for free.

Try a combination of sales, discounts and offers to see if your business volume goes up or your brand visibility is improved. Of course, a sale or a special offer cannot be eternal! This can dilute your brand value at a time when you're trying to enhance it. So be careful to do it strategically and not overdo it.

5. Public Relations

Have you sometimes wondered how an insipid designer outfit gets featured in a magazine or a particular 'upcoming' designer gets talked about a lot in the papers? Well, it's called Public Relations, baby!

After you reach a certain point in your business, it becomes incredibly important to get featured in the press and be talked about in the media. (Especially if you're looking to grow into a big brand.) Several fashion weeks, fashion festivals and contests also ask designers to submit references of their media coverage to judge popularity.

Top public relations groups charge their clients a hefty sum to keep them in the news. However, upcoming designers can find freelance public relations professionals to help spread the word too. Since PR is an ongoing effort, and it may take several attempts before even a single story about your brand appears in the papers, PR executives charge clients on a retainer basis (monthly payments).

It is not easy to determine the ideal time for you to hire a PR person. However, if you're participating in fashion weeks, have a steady stream of clients, want to get some celebrities to sport you, it is important to become a 'name' of sorts, and your PR person can help you with this.

6. 'Courtesy' Clothes

Offering your clothes on loan to models, actors, magazines, bloggers, photographers and regular people can help your marketing efforts in ways you never thought possible. Models and actors are frequently featured in interviews, events and more. Offer to lend your clothes to them for special occasions. Photographers are often doing portfolio shoots or ads that may require 'courtesy' clothing as well. Put the word out there that you can lend your clothes in return for some publicity and see what offers come up.

Of course, this is far easier to do if you live in a city like Mumbai, Delhi, Hyderabad or Chennai, where the media is vibrant and celebrity culture rampant. However, you could also offer to mail clothes to those who may need it with the understanding that they will be sent back in the same condition. A little effort in this area could provide fruitful results in getting your brand visible. By doing this, you will also get to know a lot of people in the industry and they might do you favours in return as well. (The next tip has more on this).

Since you're a young designer with shallow pockets and lots of talent, try and use the assets you have in as many ways as possible to get free publicity.

7. Good Content

While high-end traditional photo shoots and advertising campaigns grab eyeballs, they do so at costs that small businesses can scarcely afford. Even in the old days before the Internet, businesses with smaller budgets found ways to get their consumers' attention by 'making content king'. For instance, if television ad space was unaffordable, many companies created interesting radio jingles (which cost relatively little) to get a bigger bang for their buck. With the Internet and the various platforms online, the possibilities for young entrepreneurs are limitless. That said, good content is what will make you stand out, as Anita Dongre said in the beginning of this chapter.

If you're a good writer, having a well-written blog about your business can help your brand marketing efforts. Content can also mean the visual stories you tell for your brand. Do you have a business Instagram account? Are you using it to weave visual narratives about your brand?

Also, don't forget video. Get some local film students in your area to do an experimental film about your brand for free. Offer them courtesy costumes for their next production. Upload them on YouTube and other social media. Beautiful visuals, great videos and well-written content will market the hell out of your brand.

8. Fashion Bloggers

Fashion blogging in India has grown over the last few years. Upcoming fashion entrepreneurs now have a number of bloggers to reach out to. You may not be featured in *Vogue* or *Femina* just yet, but fashion blogs may be the right way to go. What's more, many fashion editors and journalists routinely check the top Indian fashion blogs to stay ahead. Getting featured there may be your first step to getting a spread in one of the many lifestyle magazines in India today.

As always, make sure your marketing strategy is well aligned with the photos and content you may share with bloggers. Also, are you ready to be featured in a national glossy? Can your business back-end handle the publicity and the demand it may lead to?

9. Get a Celeb to Sport You

An obviously smart marketing strategy is to get a celeb to sport your clothing. There are many ways you can do it, but the easiest way is to get a celebrity stylist's attention. And when we mean celebrity, we don't mean Deepika Padukone or Sonam Kapoor (unless you're in Mumbai, of course) but look for local celebrities and stylists. Getting featured in the *Pune Times* with a well-known local singer wearing your outfit is a good first step to getting featured in *Bombay Times* and eventually *Vogue* magazine! Look around; maybe your friends, or friends of friends, know singers, actors, models, musicians or performers. Spread the word and see what comes up.

10. Brand Ambassador (Psst ... For Free)

Every big business you can think of, from mobile phones to designer watches, have brand ambassadors. They are usually celebrities, artists, models or sportspersons, or in a similarly known profession. Typically, the bigger the fame and success of the brand ambassador, the higher the fee they command. That's how young cricketers in India get so rich so soon! Marketing experts recommend that the image of the brand ambassador chosen by a company should align with the values of the brand. Although many businesses fail to follow this rule, with predictably mixed results.

So how can you make this neat marketing trick work for you? Well, pay lakhs of rupees or...

Identify an upcoming celebrity, actor or other artists who get frequent media attention. Upcoming models and actors are always in need of good, designer clothes but rarely have enough work to fund their image. Help them out with your clothes, rope them in as your brand ambassador and boost your brand image. Offer them your clothes for interviews and other public appearances and in return request them to talk about your brand.

INSPIRATION — ANITA DONGRE

Mumbai-based designer Anita Dongre's AND has been around for over a decade now and retails at over 500 stores across the country. *Fortune India* featured Anita among the country's top 50 powerful women in business. Need we say more? Learn how she combined talent with marketing panache.

'I knew right at the early age of 15, that I wanted to be a fashion designer, and aspired to create a fashion empire in India. As a child, I used to spend a lot of time in my grandmother's house in Jaipur, and was completely enamoured by the beauty of Rajasthan – the colourful markets, the architecture and the people. That place ignited a creative spark in me and I decided that designing would be my chosen path. But, back in the 1990's, 'fashion design' wasn't considered a serious profession. I faced a fair share of opposition from my family members. But I was determined. After getting a degree in fashion design from SNDT College, Mumbai, I started a small workshop in my bedroom balcony with support from my sister, and started designing for friends and supplying to local boutiques.

'While a commercially viable venture, it did not satiate my creative appetite to address the fashion needs of the contemporary urban woman – a woman who sought functionality, coupled with elegance in her ensembles. I realized that most Indian women were getting their western wear tailored or buying it on their trips abroad. I wanted to address this gap and offer stylish, comfortable and accessible western-wear to them. However, while I was supplying to these boutiques, I realized that my personal creative vision was being curbed. Instead, I was being guided by the demands of the boutique owners. That made my resolution stronger to venture out on my own and start my own western-wear label.

'Seeing my unrelenting passion, my father gave in and offered me a loan to start a small factory of my own. That laid the foundation for my fashion house ADIL in 1998 and I started my first brand, AND, which was launched in 1999, at Mumbai's first ever mall, Crossroad.

'When I started AND in 1999, it was the first Indian, high-fashion brand in the western wear category. Even with a first mover advantage, we realized the need for an effective marketing campaign to establish the brand's identity, its position as a category leader, to inform, persuade, motivate and remind the consumer about the brand and its benefits. With the economy opening up, and the influx of so many international brands, the consumer is spoilt for choice, the competition just gets fiercer, and you end up competing for a single target consumer's mind space. Hence, in such a scenario, 'marketing' communication becomes a critical tool to reinforce the 'point of differentiation' or simply put, the brand USP vis-a-vis the brand's competitors.'

3-POINT ACTION PLAN (SYNCHRONIZE YOUR BRAND AND MARKETING STRATEGY)

1. Work on Your Brand Values

Make a list of all the words that come to your mind when you think of your brand (this list can be in any language). Keep thinking of these words when you have the time, when you're commuting, having a shower, designing ... whenever you can. Over a period of time (perhaps two or three weeks), make a final list of five words that represent your brand.

2. Brand Value Test

Every time you make an effort to market your brand, put it to the brand value test. For instance, if your brand values are youthful, edgy, creative, innovative and cool, does your website reflect the exact same values? Are your Instagram uploads cool, edgy, creative? Keeping asking yourself if your marketing communication accurately reflects your brand values. Eventually, you will start doing this intuitively.

3. Unique Ideas

Now that you have a list of brand values, start thinking of marketing ideas that reflect your values. Once again, if youthful, edgy, creative, innovative and cool are your brand values, can you think of marketing ideas to support them? For instance, can you make an edgy, creative video and upload it on YouTube and share it as widely as you can?

6

Your Big Brand Fashion Label

I have some good news: we're half way into our journey of understanding the various aspects of setting up a fashion business! By now, you should have at least a broad understanding of several key areas of fashion designing and entrepreneurship, including the process of designing clothes, marketing your brand, and registering your brand name. In this chapter, I'll introduce you to the various stages of manufacturing that fashion entrepreneurs go through.

Many designers start out manufacturing from their homes with one tailor, and go on to set up workshops that employ over a hundred people. It is crucial for you to have some reference points as you go through your own journey of manufacturing clothes for your label. Setting up a manufacturing unit, even if it includes just two or three people, is not an easy task. If you start this at home, you may find it disrupts your work-life balance. However, many designers start with such a meagre budget that they don't have the luxury of choice. Nonetheless, as your business grows, you can scale up your manufacturing, beginning with finding a location to do so.

ECONOMY OF SCALE A.K.A. INDUSTRIAL REVOLUTION

The volume of clothes you produce will depend on the segment you cater to. For instance, your specialty may be couture, in which case you will not be producing 100 outfits a day. A designer who works in the field of pret, however, who retails at hundreds of outlets, may produce over 100 outfits a day in a factory. Few designers produce clothes in small volumes and eventually most scale their operations to manufacture large quantities. Generally speaking, manufacturing clothes or accessories is done on an industrial scale.

One often hears the word 'industrial' used with manufacturing and production. Industrial production means the same as manufacturing, i.e. production of large volumes of products with the use of machinery.

If you're used to browsing through history books, you'll know about the Industrial Revolution. It may sound a little boring, but it is interesting to know and may even be useful for your business. In the 19th century, most of the Western world went through massive industrialization, where several goods went from being manufactured in a small scale by people to being manufactured in a large scale by machines. This had a huge impact on the fashion industry. For instance, instead of people spinning fabrics for clothes, where a meter could take a whole day, machines spun fabrics in no time. Today, if you place the order for 10,000 pieces of a simple T-shirt design, you may get it in a week's time.

EXPLORE!

Google 'Industrial Revolution + Fashion' to know more about how industrialization shaped the fashion industry

---

as we know it today, from designing to production to distribution. Don't feel like reading? Search 'industrial revolution' on YouTube, you'll find several five- to ten-minute videos explaining the era to you. It'll help you understand how many aspects of the business you will be working on have been shaped.

STAGES OF MANUFACTURING – THE ENTREPRENEURIAL JOURNEY

Tailor – The One-Man Show

Many of the designers we spoke to for this book started off with a good tailor in their home studios, including famous designers such as JJ Valaya and Anita Dongre. This should give aspiring designers like you some hope.

If your one and only employee is going to be a master tailor, make sure he or she is really good at his work. Finding a good tailor will require a bit of effort and ingenuity. This means looking in every place possible. Call friends, ask well-dressed people, find a contact at an export house, approach tailors in your locality, etc. Few people are lucky enough to stumble upon their master tailor in the first attempt. Keep trying and eventually you'll land that dream master tailor for your label.

Small Unit

Some businesses are not yet brand names but are getting there. They do not have enough business to place big volume orders with garment manufacturers but will absolutely drive the rest of the family crazy if they continue to run their business from home. The solution: a small business unit. Not quite a full-fledged studio or workshop but not a one-person show either.

Designers will have to be creative while running a small business unit, because renting a premise and hiring three to five tailors and embroiders may not be economical in the long run. Another option could be to set up a small unit in collaboration with another designer, or hire a small team at an export house during lean months, or even to create a sub-unit at a big tailoring shop. A small unit is a step towards a bigger workshop or outsourcing large-volume production.

Young fashion designers may find this phase particularly stressful. You may suddenly have to deal with labour issues, your account books may begin to look fiendishly complex, or you may have wavering business cycles, from extremely busy to extremely sluggish. Also, what happens if you decide to suddenly shut your small business unit down and outsource?

The Factories Act (1948) and its amendments regulates small units. If you have more than ten workers, ensure that you comply with all the stipulations laid out by the Factories Act. Consult a lawyer to help you with the same.

Outsourcing

Many big designers outsource production during their growth phase. However, they switch back to having their own studio once their growth has stabilized and they're an established brand name.

Outsourcing makes sense as it frees you from dealing with employees and the other hassles that come with managing a production unit. However, outsourcing does come at a cost and you have to do the calculations to ensure your business can afford it. Once you're confident that your business is ready, it's time to talk to a manufacturer. While there are many garment manufacturers in India, you may discover that finding a comprehensive list of them is not easy. Start by talking to friends and family with connections in the manufacturing business as a first step.

However, you may also get lucky with listings on B2B (business to business service provider) sites like www.indiamart. com, where garment manufacturers are listed alongside other service providers. You could also try reaching out to members of the Clothing Manufacturers Association of India (CMAI) for advice on finding the best manufacturer for you.

Designer Tanya Sharma says, 'I have been outsourcing my production for a long time because having a studio is quite expensive. You can't have a workshop right from the beginning. Your outgoings [rent, utilities, salaries, etc.] will be nothing less than a lakh a month. So many big designers I know started off by outsourcing. Once you know you're getting good returns, you can invest in your own studio.'

Workshop/Studio

Most top Indian designers, especially the ones designing couture and bridal wear, run their own manufacturing units. While this is expensive, it gives designers almost a 100 per cent control over the manufacturing process. From ensuring that the right quality of fabrics are used, to ensuring the embellishments are what you envisioned, even to safeguarding original designs, an in-house studio offers many advantages to designers of a certain level and makes the cost well worth it. Of course, top designers are also able to afford production managers and other team members who make sure their production units run smoothly. This leaves them free to focus on their designing and taking active part in other aspects of their business that they might enjoy – such as marketing, working with celebrity brand ambassadors and even shooting their own brand campaigns.

After starting his business out of his dining room, today JJ Valaya has his own sprawling work studio. Being successful means that his team takes care of all the management issues, which gives him time to pursue his hobbies, like painting and also photography. He is also able to focus on diversifying and growing his business, such as curating luxury home décor for India's discerning decorators and home-owners. Reaching this stage has taken him twenty years. Younger designers could aspire to reach this point sooner, depending on various factors.

OUTSOURCING ABROAD – IS IT FOR INDIANS?

If you decide to scour the Internet for manufacturers, you will find a lot of information catering to designers in America or the U.K., where manufacturing has slowed down with the advent of outsourcing. You may find a lot of information pertaining to manufacturers in India, catering to international designers. You can start from there and see if these manufacturers will work with you. However, if you can't find good options in India, you may be tempted to seek manufacturers in other countries like China, Bangladesh or Sri Lanka.

If you stumble upon an extremely well-organized manufacturing business based out of China and find that even with the shipping and delivery costs accounted for, the cut, finish and style they offer are unmatchable in India, by all means, go for it! Most of these businesses are used to taking orders over the Internet and have enough processes in place to ensure your orders go through smoothly. You may also be surprised to find similar options in India if you look hard enough.

If it's purely business, and it is viable for you, by all means explore the option of outsourcing your manufacturing needs abroad. However, if you want to encourage local manufacturers and contribute to the local economy, you may find several competitive Indian production options. Do remember that outsourcing involves complying with technical file formats and other requirements; you may need to hire a design assistant to do this for you.

People Management for Small Businesses

Managing people, especially if you're a young entrepreneur, can be quite a task. Once you've set up a small manufacturing unit and have a group of people with different personalities working together, you will find that managing ego clashes and other problems of that nature will become a part of your job. You will need to start learning how to manage time very well – both your own and that of those who work for you, so that you don't lose focus from your larger goal.

In Chapter 3, there are more tips from designers themselves, on hiring and people management. You could consider several options; take a free online Human Resource/Personnel Management course, or even reach out and chat with a well-established entrepreneur you may know to find out how she handled problems in this area. Being patient and learning on the job is, of course, always an option.

You might also, after doing the accounts, realize that you can afford to delegate people management to a manager within the unit. If that is the case, do so. This means you will just be dealing with and managing two or three people, such as the unit manager, the master tailor and perhaps an assistant.

People management is very important for entrepreneurs and will help take the business forward. Rest assured that as your business grows, you will be able to afford to delegate many chores. This will liberate you to be the free-spirited, creative designer you were meant to be, while also being a successful entrepreneur.

WHAT IS PRICING AND COSTING? WHAT IS THE DIFFERENCE?

This is the slightly boring 'business-side' of the business – everything to do with numbers, accounts, the bottom line, etc. But here's a good way to look at it: doing this right (and provided a few other factors go your way) can help you establish a profitable business. As a successful entrepreneur, you will be your own boss, and can manage your time and money the way you want to. That's a great reward for spending some time understanding pricing and costing.

I promise: once you've read this, you will realize that you instinctively understand the idea. Everybody does, from the roadside chaiwallah to the guy who sells cheap fancy slippers, to big label design brands.

Pricing

Simply put, pricing is the process of fixing the selling price for your products. You will price your clothes to be sold to retailers or to sell them directly at your own store or e-commerce store. Pricing your garments is a multi-step process. Thousands of businesses are set up every year and go through a similar process of pricing their goods, so understanding it is not that hard.

Costing

Costing, in simple terms, means the amount that making the garments costs you. To arrive at the right cost, you have to take into account every conceivable expenditure you have incurred to produce your garments. You will take into account the fabric, the threads, the embellishments like buttons and embroidery, labour costs and overheads.

Yes, it sounds complex but once you get the hang of it, it will be easy. Needless to say, you will need an accountant to help you get through this process. There is simply no way out of this but to get expert help. However, here is a brief idea of how setting a price in the fashion industry works.

Please note: This table does not follow industry standards or use technical terms common in the fashion industry. It is simplified to give you an idea of how pricing works.

Costing Break-up of Producing 100 T-shirts

Item	Price (Rs)
Fabric	10,000
Embellishments	5,000
Washing	1,000
Packaging	1,000
Labour	3,000
Transport	3,000
Total	**23,000**

So the total cost (TC) of producing 100 T-shirts is Rs 23,000. Now, you decide the wholesale price (the amount you charge the retailer). Let's say the wholesale price (WP) is Rs 35,000. You decide to sell the 100 T-shirts to the retailer at Rs 35,000 or Rs 350 per T-shirt.

Your profit is WP minus TC, i.e. Rs 35,000 − Rs 23,000 = Rs 12,000. (The retailer will sell the 100 T-shirts for a retail price [MRP] of Rs 65,000.)

But why or how did you decide to sell the T-shirts for Rs 350? Let's look at the following section for answers.

FACTORS TO CONSIDER WHEN SETTING A PRICE

Cost to Price

This is a simple way to price a product and is illustrated above. You simply decide that you need a certain percentage of profit on your total cost and price accordingly. You take this decision on different factors, such as how much you need to sustain your business and produce more products.

Brand Values

The price you set for your product will also be determined by the brand values you've adopted for a particular line or your entire business. For instance, if you're a youth brand and are primarily targeting college students, you can't price your product too expensively. You will have to take into account not only the price at which you sell the product to the retailer but also the retailer's 'mark-up' (i.e. the higher price that the retailers assign to a product to make a profit).

EXPLORE!

Ever wondered why luxury goods cost so much? Or how certain luxury brands can get away by charging so much for so little? Read the Wikipedia entry about 'Veblen Goods'. Veblen (Thorstein Veblen) was an economist who said that luxury products are bought because they are expensive. Thus decreasing the price of a product, perceived to be luxurious or exclusive, can affect its sales. Google terms: 'Veblen Good' + 'Wikipedia'.

Consumer Expectations

Another important factor to consider when setting your price is to understand consumer expectations. Forget for a second that you're a fashion designer and entrepreneur. Think of yourself as a consumer. Let's talk about your expectations as a potential buyer of a smartphone. You're looking for a basic smartphone with good memory, a bunch of extra features and sleek design. How much would you pay for it? We'll take a guess here: About Rs 25,000. Now, imagine you find a phone with exactly all the features you want – no less, no more – but costing Rs 70,000. Woah! What a bummer, right? You're never going to buy that phone. What's worse is, you come out of the store really angry that the company wants to charge you so much for a basic smartphone.

You can apply the same process when it comes to pricing your product. Put yourself in the shoes of the consumer and imagine what he or she is used to paying for products in your category. You may want to consider this before setting the price of your product.

Consumer's Perceived Value

Obviously, there are opportunities to make bigger profits, depending on what you have to offer consumers. Do you have a unique idea? For instance, are you selling super-comfortable yet super-chic maternity wear? In that case, stylish mothers-to-be may be willing to pay a premium for your outfits. This is the 'perceived' value, and adds value to your clothes over what it costs to produce them. Designing and producing an awesome top for moms-to-be may not be that expensive, but given that these are hard to come by, consumers will value them more and hence maybe willing to pay more for them. If you offer unique, interesting, unusual, fantastically designed outfits, you may be able to get away with pricing your products higher.

Market Conditions

It is very important for entrepreneurs to understand market conditions. This can affect every area of their business, from launching a new collection to hiring more people and even to pricing. If there is a recession, consumers will be shopping far less than usual. On the other hand, you may have a unique idea that will help you sell more during a recession, such as affordable designer wear. Stay tuned to market conditions and you'll be able to tailor your prices appropriately.

Competition

Who are your competitors? How much are they charging for their products? Can you afford to charge as much? Sometimes, big brands produce in larger volumes and can afford to charge far less than independent fashion labels would. Understand the market and the competition well before you price your products.

Costing

We touched upon costing briefly in one of the sections. Let's take another look. Here we are costing garments produced over a season (three months) and arriving at costs per garment. Most businesses will arrive at the total cost of the garments by adding their total expenses and dividing it by number of garments produced. Following is an illustration for your understanding.

Please note: This does not meet industry standards and does not use technical terms often used by the fashion industry. It is simplified for your reference only.

Costing for Period of June, July and August 2016

Item	Price (Rs)
Fabric	2,00,000
Embellishments	50,000
Washing	15,000
Packaging	20,000
Labour	50,000
Transport	20,000
Total Cost (TC)	**3,55,000**

Let's say the total number (TN) of garments produced during the period June, July and August was 150. Now, divide total cost (TC = Rs 3,55,000) by total number (TN = 150).

The result is Rs 2,366. Therefore, each outfit costs you Rs 2,366 to produce.

Of course, keep in mind that not all garments are the same. Some demand hours of labour, others may be really simple to produce. After arriving at a standard cost for each garment, you will have to categorize your line and cost them separately before pricing all your garments.

Costing Per Garment

Here's a rough example of how you would break-up a single piece of garment to cost it. In the first pricing chart, we showed you how you can add up total costs and divide it by the number of garments produced. Here's another way to do it.

Garment type: Women's embroidered T-shirt. Now, make a list of all the expenses you incurred to make the T-shirt. For instance, cost of:

1. Jersey fabric used in T-shirt, per kg
2. Weight of T-shirt (before embellishments, etc., to figure out rough cost of fabric used per T-shirt)
3. Labour cost
4. Embroidery thread
5. Embellishments: buttons and beads
6. CMT costs (cut, make and trim) if outsourced to factories; labour charges if done internally.

Please note: This break-up is not as per industry standards and is simplified for easy understanding.

Profit

Cost of production subtracted from the total income from sales leaves your profit. However, an established fashion label may have other sources of income such as brand tie-ups, merchandising (creating accessories based on a fast-selling collection, for instance), brand expansion (JJ Valaya has created Valaya Homes where products chosen by Mr Valaya are sold), and so on.

3-POINT ACTION PLAN

1. Manufacturing

Can you find a contact – a friend, a family member, an acquaintance – just about anybody to connect you with a manufacturing unit in your city? You can go along with a friend and ask the manager to explain the process to you. The next best thing to this experience is a tailoring unit. In any case, a home-run label's production will resemble that of a tailoring unit more than a full-fledged manufacturing studio. Try and get a feel for the manufacturing process. It can help expand your mind across several areas including design, budgeting and labour management.

2. Costing

Identify three outfits of your choice for this exercise, preferably outfits that you remember how much you paid for. Now, based on the simplified method provided in this chapter, create a cost break-up of each of those outfits. Based on the cost break-up, can you guess the wholesale and the retail price of the outfit? What were the retailer's margins? How much did the designer/ label make on each of those outfits?

3. Pricing

For this exercise, take the same three outfits. Now that you know how much the outfit costs to make and how much it was actually sold for, can you identify the pricing strategy that the label used to price the clothes? Look through the 'Factors to Consider When Pricing' section of this chapter, can you find any of the factors mentioned as the reason for pricing the outfits?

7

MONEY!

It's all very well to chase your dream, follow your heart, and set up your own fashion label, but where are you going to get the money for it? To set up your own business, you need money to invest in equipment, labour, marketing and more. You also need enough to cover your own living expenses from month to month. That's why this chapter is so crucial.

Here's how you can make the most of the information here.

1. Read the seven methods listed below.
2. Make a list of methods that you think are most applicable to you.
3. Research and discuss these with friends and family. Plan and work out a strategy to fund your business by one or more of the methods listed here.

Good Luck!

METHOD ONE: COLLATERAL-FREE LOANS

Several nationalized and private banks in India offer collateral-free loans to entrepreneurs. 'Collateral-free' basically means you don't have to hand over the papers to property, FD receipts or other investments such as jewellery in order to secure a loan. Banks typically need some sort of surety (protection should you not be able to repay the loan offered) and ask for collateral. In case you default, they will get their money back by selling your collateral.

Collateral-free loans are a great opportunity for entrepreneurs like you to find funding for your vision and ideas. However, these loans are not *entirely* collateral-free. All the assets that you create out of the loan will belong to the bank, and in case of default or non-payment of instalments, the bank has the right to seize your assets. This could be the machines and other equipment you buy for your studio, fabrics, etc.

If you're a woman, banks in India offer several concessions such as lower interest rate, lower margins and more. But this is not to discourage the men, as with a good business plan and vision, you can secure a loan and get set to start your business too.

Caution

1. It is often hard to convince bank managers, who disburse loans at their discretion, to give unsecured loans to entrepreneurs in creative fields. It is up to you to create a business plan (check Chapter 2 on guidelines to create one) and present it to the bank convincingly.

2. Since banks are increasingly more pressured to support entrepreneurship and small enterprises, funds are usually earmarked for this purpose. If you ensure that your application is upto the mark and demonstrates that your business will succeed or, at the very least, create enough

assets for the bank to recover their funds in case of a loss, your application may be successful.

3. Sometimes, banks may also ask for a 'Third Party' guarantee with enough funds and sources of income, so they may recover their money from them in case you default on payments. This usually leaves those keen on securing a loan asking friends and relatives for favours.

4. No legitimate bank will offer you 100 per cent credit. You will have put down some 'margin money' or 'down payment', anywhere from 15 per cent to 25 per cent of the loan that you want to secure. So you may have to save some money or have somebody lend you the 'margin money' before you can secure the rest of the amount from the bank.

METHOD TWO – LOANS WITH COLLATERAL

Collateral loans are relatively easier to secure for creative and unusual business ideas like fashion design than collateral-free loans. However, a good business plan is still important, not just to convince the bank but also yourself that your business will generate the kind of money that can keep you going in the long run. If you have assets such as property or investments and are looking for larger loans (exceeding Rs 1 crore, for instance) you may be able to secure a loan against the collateral.

You can also use collateral to secure working capital for your business. That is, the money you require to continue to keep your business in the market. Some banks may require that your business has been up and running for years (sometimes three or more) and must have been profit-making at least for a year. Loans with collateral give you the option of securing funding for your expansion plans, working capital or possibly, even to set up your business without selling your assets. You may not want to sell heirloom jewellery or property that has been in your family for generations to fund your business. In this case, approach a bank.

Caution

1. While loans with collateral may be relatively easy to secure, remember that you're risking your assets. The bank essentially controls your assets as long as you owe them money.

2. Several non-banking organizations offer loans against collateral, such as gold, and these loans are not specifically geared to business owners; but you will be able to get the money you require. Many small entrepreneurs take this route as this means less documentation, and sometimes, more money. But there's greater risk here: no one asks for your business plan or why you need the money. This means you don't have another set of objective eyes looking at your plans. Also, it is entirely upto you to decide how you spend that money as long as you pay the instalments or are okay with the bank seizing your assets!

DO IT!

No matter what stage of business you are in, enquiring about loan schemes at banks doesn't hurt. Can you make an appointment with your local bank branch or walk in and enquire about their business loans?

Remember, however, that they may ask you questions about your business. Perhaps, it will be good to have a draft of your business plan to ensure you have a good professional experience. There's no better way to learn about the funding opportunities than go out on the field and gather information!

METHOD THREE – CREDIT CARDS

No, we don't mean you max out the credit card that you got when you were last working to set up your business. Luckily, banks these days offer business credit cards geared exclusively for small business owners. Of course, this means you already must have a business set-up. (Yes, nothing is easy in the world of securing funding!) You can use your business credit card for the smaller needs of running your everyday business, such as buying a set of new sewing machines. Or, funds to deliver an order for which no advance payment has been made and you're tight on capital.

The credit limit for business credit cards vary from business to business, depending on your size, assets and other factors. Business credit cards also offer advantages like converting your purchases into monthly EMIs and also securing a loan against the card.

With credit scores becoming increasingly important in India, it makes sense to keep your personal credit card exclusively for your personal use and secure an additional business credit card, especially if you find yourself depending on your personal card or other personal sources of funding for your monthly business expenses. This also means you don't have to scour through several personal bank accounts and credit statements to help your accountant maintain your business books.

Caution

1. As cautious as they are when it comes to offering loans, banks are pushy when it comes to credit card sales. You may be able to get a business credit card relatively easily; make sure you use all its advantages and are disciplined about using it solely for the business and that you are making regular payments to clear your account.
2. If you get more than one card for your business, you must ensure that you trust the employees you're handing the business credit card to. Any misuse or litigation that might follow could affect your business credit score.
3. Needless to say, make sure you sign up for a credit card with a reputed bank only. Credit cards do not typically need assets or collateral. Steer clear of any credit card offers that ask you for these.
4. Finally, even the best, most trustworthy bank will be largely unsympathetic when it comes to recovering its assets. Therefore, the responsibility of handling your credit facilities in a disciplined manner is entirely in your hands.

Government Schemes

The Indian government has several schemes geared exclusively for small and medium enterprises. In fact, the loans that nationalized banks offer businesses are thanks to the many Indian government schemes and recent laws that have been passed with an eye to favouring small businesses and spurring manufacturing. Go through the several schemes that the government has launched to support small businesses to understand your funding options better. (Link in the 'Explore!' note.)

The loans that you may intend to secure through banks are offered through 'apex bodies' that the government has set up, such as Small Industries Development Organisation (SIDCO) and National Small Industries Corporation Limited (NSIC).

Here's why you should know about the government schemes:

1. The Indian government offers certain standard regulations to banks and other financial institutions when it comes to lending. This means that almost all banks will use the same criteria to assess whether your business plan or needs are viable and will generate profits for you as well as the bank. Understanding these rules is a first step to securing your loan. Then, you can create a shortlist of a few banks based on accessibility and how professionally you feel the local branch is run (this varies widely), and approach them with your application. Knowing the rules in advance and knowing that you will find similar eligibility criteria across banks can help you prepare your documentation accordingly. This also prevents you from running to several banks with a weak application and wondering why they are all rejecting your idea.

2. Looking through the various schemes that the government has launched also helps you understand your rights as an aspiring entrepreneur in India today. While it is true that loans are typically approved at the discretion of the bank manager, it is also a fact that you are entitled to the funds that the government apex bodies set aside for small businesses – provided you meet all the criteria. Knowing your rights means being confident in your ability to get funds for your business. While you may not want to challenge uncooperative bank

managers or bank branches, you can choose to move on to the others and find a more willing partner.

EXPLORE!

Look through the Government of India's resourceful and well-designed website catering exclusively for the information needs of entrepreneurs like you: www. business.gov.in (The site has been archived and can be accessed by searching the address – business.gov. in through Google). It covers the whole gamut, from starting a business to registering a company to, of course, funding. Click the 'Business Finance' link on the homepage and access the Government Schemes section. Want to get to it faster? Google 'Government + India + Schemes + Funding + Businesses'. Find the 'gov.in' site listed in the search results. This should show up at the top.

The business.gov.in site should also take you to the funding apex bodies' sites. Here they are in case you want to go directly:

www.nsic.co.in: On the homepage you will find the link to 'schemes', which will explain in detail the funding that NSIC makes available to banks for small business like yours. It even offers links to various well-known banks. You can start your search from here. In addition, the NSIC site offers other resources that you may be interested in.

SIDCO: You can reach the SIDCO site through the link on the Funding page in business.gov.in. Once again, it has various resources and information that can help you with your loan application. Also, Googling terms like 'SIDCO + India + Business' can lead you to various regional SIDCOs (such as Kerala SIDCO), which offer more region-based information.

Keep Your Papers Ready

Here's a standard list of documents required for loans, business credit cards, government scheme funds, etc.

1. Income Tax returns for the last two to three financial years.
2. Business Account demonstrating profit and loss, as well as Income and Balance Sheet (a chartered accountant should help you with this).
3. Business Bank Account Statement for the last six months.
4. Business Registration and other documents as proof of existence.
5. Others, depending on the lender.

This is a basic list. In addition to these documents, you may be asked to submit others as well. Get ready to prepare a nice thick file of different documents – the requirements could vary from lender to lender. Please also note that new businesses applying for loans to start their business may have to provide personal bank and tax statements.

METHOD FOUR – VENTURE CAPITAL

Venture Capital, or VC as it known, is a great way to get an organized, professional form of investment for your business. Venture capitalists (VCs) are basically serial investors looking for interesting, energetic business ideas to invest in. More often than not, VCs are associated with technology-based businesses or businesses that rely on technology or the web. However, an original, innovative idea can find VC funding. Shailesh's Singh's Seed Fund invested in an online fashion company that designs their clothes in-house and sells their clothes exclusively online. This is a great idea for an aspiring fashion designer and entrepreneur.

'We look for great business with large potential and great teams which can execute those plans well. The thing that matters in fashion is traction. Traction in this can be the buzz and trend it is creating. The key thing is that it is not another boutique label but something which can define fashion,' he says. If you have a truly unique fashion-design based idea, perhaps you could find VC funding.

Caution

VC funding is not for every business. As Shailesh says, 'VC investments are good only for those where there are "exit-able" opportunities. There are a lot of good businesses but they are not what we call VC businesses. However, VC/PE (private equity) investors do regularly invest in the fashion industry.'

EXPLORE!

Whether or not you have a unique business idea worthy of VC investment, understanding how VCs and PEs work will help you gain valuable insights about the fashion industry and understand the market better. If these words sound like Latin or Sanskrit to you, rest assured that there is nothing complicated to the matter. They

---

work on a simple idea of 'we give you money and we will take some of your profits'. So absolutely no need to be intimidated!

Google terms: 1. 'Private Equity + India + Fashion/ Fashion industry'

2. 'Venture Capital + India + Fashion/Fashion/ industry'. Also read the Wikipedia entries on 'Private Equity' and 'Venture Capital' if interested.

METHOD FIVE – PRIVATE EQUITY

Like VC funding, private equity offers businesses a systematic, organized form of investment. However, they fund directly and do not buy stocks or equity of the company. They do not buy publicly traded companies (companies that are listed on the stock market).

Caution

Before you pick up the phone and start calling private equity investors, we must caution you that it'll probably not work out for you at this point. PEs, as they are known, will rarely show interest in new businesses, particularly in the fashion business, and those in India. For instance, one of the few fashion-based private equity investments in India was in designer Ritu Kumar's eponymous label. Kumar holds the 'Padma Shri' title, among the highest honours conferred by the Indian government to civilians, and has been in the fashion business for over twenty-five years.

This should give you a fair idea of the kinds of businesses that PEs are typically interested in! However, it is important for you to understand how financing works if you're looking for funding. Besides, it may not necessarily take you over two decades to build the kind of fashion business that PEs may be interested in! It's always good to know your options – just in case.

METHOD SIX – FAMILY LOANS

I have listed several options above, and as exciting as many of them seem, it's perhaps time for a reality check. The fashion industry, while booming, is still seen as a risky investment. There might be a great deal of coverage in the media about fashion and the industry in general, but not everybody in the business is able to break into the big league or rake in the big moolah easily. Therefore, loans and investments from the formal banking and investment sector may be out of bounds to many aspiring fashion designers. This may change in a few years, but who wants to wait forever, right? Many of the investors we interviewed for the book relied on their family to offer them that first loan to get started.

'Back in the 1990s, 'fashion design' wasn't considered a serious profession, and I faced a fair share of opposition from my family members. But I was determined, and started a small workshop in my bedroom balcony with support from my sister, and started designing for friends and supplying to boutiques. Seeing my unrelenting passion, my father gave in and offered me a loan to start a small factory of my own. That laid the foundation of my fashion house ADIL in 1998 and I started my first brand, AND, which was launched in 1999,' says fashion designer Anita Dongre. (You can read more by Anita Dongre in the 'Inspiration' section of Chapter 5.) You may also have to rely on your family for a loan to start your business.

Caution

1. As always, no matter where your loan or investment comes from, there are risks associated with it. Is borrowing from your family a good idea? It all depends on the equation you share with them and the trust they have in you. Do you think your family will poke their noses in your business affairs because they gave you that money? (It happens.) Or perhaps, you come from a middle-class family and the fashion business is far too risky for you to pour your parents' savings into? It is for you to decide – if you think it's the right decision, go ahead and present your business plan to them.

2. Explore other options before seeking a family loan. A loan from a bank will mean you will be more disciplined about the repayments and also ensure that you work towards creating a profitable business sooner rather than later. Once again, this varies from person to person. You will have to decide on the best possible option not just for your business but also for your personal relationships. A transfer of money between close relatives or friends more often than not brings about a shift in the equation.

METHOD SEVEN – INCREMENTAL INVESTMENTS

Many of the designers interviewed for this book continued to reinvest their income from their fledgling fashion business for expansion and growth. This could be an alternative for designers with good start-up capital from family, savings or a small loan. So every quarter, six months or annually, you keep a portion of your business profits to invest in your workshop, studio or enhancing your own skills as a designer by taking up a course or doing an apprenticeship or even entering a fashion week.

Tanya Sharma has won accolades at the Lakme India Fashion Week year after year and was shortlisted for the Vogue Fashion Fund's Rs 25 lakh cash award in 2013. She didn't win the award but she did get great reviews and support for her label 'Gaga' from the editorial team. That in itself is a huge achievement, but a new label demands constant financial support. 'I launched it with the money I saved working as a model. Even now, it's hard to sustain the label just by sales. I also work as a stylist for ad films, photo shoots, etc., and invest back all the money into the label. That's how I am growing it right now. It's working for now. But I am also in talks with some investors who'll help me expand at a faster pace,' she says.

Caution

This is a slower way to growth but a steady and common path that many fashion designers take. You may find that you're constantly juggling funds to keep your business growing for a few years, until you're set up. If your business has been steadily profitable, you don't have to do this, as you can secure working capital loans from banks.

WILDCARD METHOD EIGHT – COMPETITIONS

Several international and a few national competitions for fashion designers offer cash prizes. Keep an eye out for competitions and send in your entries. Try your luck – what's the worst that can happen? In either case, you will wind up fine-tuning your design ideas and adding new outfits to your portfolio. Some of the famous annual international competitions for fashion designers are International Talent Support (ITS) Fashion Competition, Mango Fashion Awards and International Design Awards. In India, Vogue Fashion Fund is emerging as one of the biggest competitions for fashion designers.

Caution

1. Obviously, banking on a competitive fashion design contest to fund your business is not an entirely prudent idea. If you do win the competition, however, you get much more than money. For instance, the Diesel Fashion Awards (2014) offers a cash prize of 25,000 euros. Of course, the money will go a long way in helping your business but imagine what winning a prestigious, global design contest can do for your label!

2. International awards are extremely competitive and award-based support for creative professionals and entrepreneurs within India is unfortunately still rare.

INSPIRATION — JJ VALAYA

Jagsharanjit Singh Ahluwalia was training to be a chartered accountant when he realized he absolutely did not want to become one. He decided to give it up and wrote the entrance exam for National Institute of Fashion Technology and got through. It is so clichéd to say this, but sometimes there's no better alternative — the rest is history and the JJ Valaya brand was born.

'I come from an Army family, so I had a very different upbringing. We're in a constant state of flux.

We leave cities, friends and memories behind year after year. So although it seemed like a radical decision that I was leaving a very secure career in accountancy and I didn't know what I wanted to do at the time, it wasn't that much of a big deal.

'Initially, my family was a little surprised and then they said, 'Okay, then figure out what you want to do, so you don't have any regrets later.'

'The first best decision of my life was quitting the training to be a chartered accountant and the second best decision of my life was starting my own label. Here's how it happened. When you're just about to graduate, you introspect on what is it that you really want to do. Ashish Soni was a close friend of mine at NIFT (Soni is a famous designer in his own right today). We were hanging around on the campus and talking about what we wanted to do. We decided to flip a coin. Heads meant we would work somewhere and tails meant each one would start his respective label. And that was it! I decided to do it.

'As a student I had won an award in Paris (The Prix d'Incitation at the Paris-based Young Designers International Competition). It came with a cash prize of Rs 26,000. I used some of that money to buy my first car – a second-hand Maruti! The rest went into my business. But that wasn't enough. I took a small loan of Rs 10,000 from my father. At that time, my brother left the army to join me and he got his Provident Fund and other cash settlements. So all this money came together and became my "start-up" capital.'

8

Your Clothes at a Big Store

If you're a newbie or wannabe (there's nothing wrong with that word, by the way) designer, you may think of this word – shops – when you think of shopping. It's time for you to transition from a creative person, designer, student, wannabe (we love that word!) and take another step towards thinking like an entrepreneur.

Start thinking 'retail'. Simply speaking, retail is just the corporate/business-world way of saying shops. As you begin to establish your fashion-design business, you will start getting obsessed with this and related words – retail, retailing, retail price, etc. Because where you sell your clothes and how much you sell will determine your profits and ultimately, the health of your business.

Let's start with a basic introduction to the different kinds of retail stores that aspiring designers can target to market and sell their products.

TYPES OF RETAIL STORES

Independent Boutiques

These are boutiques run by entrepreneurs who source clothes from a variety of places. This could include a select number of imports from small brands in Asia or elsewhere, designs by local, upcoming designers, clothes designed in-house and tailored locally, or a combination of all of this. No-brand designers with some great ideas have a good of chance selling their clothes here. But the quality and nature of an independent boutique can only be assessed from local reputation.

Many independent boutiques across the country are run by entrepreneurs with no design background but a great sense of fashion and style. They have regular clientele that flock to them for their fashion fix. Other so-called boutiques could just be dumping grounds for export rejects or overpriced tailoring shops.

Multi-brand Department Store

There are several department stores in India that sell a variety of products under one roof. This could include clothes, toys, shoes, household items, etc. A few examples are Shoppers' Stop, Westside and Central. Many designers who make clothes that fit the budget and category of clothes available at these stores might dream of seeing their garments stocked here. It is possible with some time and effort. Several designers like Anita Dongre and Biba's Mina Bindra started small and now sell at these multi-brand stores. Their clothes are available in almost every major city in the country via those same department stores.

Multi-designer Store

These are high-end stores, typically seen at some of the major metros. The number and variety of designers available may vary, however, the idea is to sell the best designer clothes and accessories to those who can afford it. Every big city has its own designer luxury store, if not several of them. Mumbai is famous for Kimaya and now this store can be found in other cities too. Ffolio is well-known among Bangalore's glitterati, while Hyderabad's Banjara Hills is chock-a-block with high-end designer stores. Some of the biggest stores such as Kimaya have a wide range of designers on display, with upcoming Indian, Pakistani and South African designers jostling for space with international designer brands such as Michael Kors, Versace, Armani Jeans, etc. Needless to say Delhi, Kolkata and Chennai all have their own designer boutiques too.

DO IT!

Do you live in a biggish city? Can you make a list of the designer stores in your city and visit them? If possible, make it a habit to visit at least once every two months. It's one thing to look at stuff on the Internet, it's another to actually see what is being displayed and sold every season. If you don't have access to these stores, don't fret. Go out there and check out your local multi-brand store and independent boutiques.

Flagship Store

A flagship store is one of the main stores of a designer or a brand. For most designers, the moment they set up their flagship store is both special and unforgettable. Stand-alone stores are similar in idea, in that they sell only one brand. However, flagship stores will have chains across the city, region or the country. It is meant to be the best in some way – either the designer works there or visits frequently, or the store is the biggest and gets the newest designs first.

'We started our first flagship store in Delhi in 1996. This was nearly eighteen years back and the area of Chhatarpur, where we set up the store, was not developed at all. We had opened in the middle of a farm! It was set on one acre of land,' says couturier JJ Valaya about his first flagship store. 'The store had a café, an art gallery, an interior's section, and of course, our clothes. We christened the store "JJ Valaya Life". We ran that store for fifteen years. We never had signages or boards. Anybody who wanted us reached us there. I still remember the opening day. It was a Herculean task just getting there, all the way from the city. But a large number of people turned up. Everybody was flummoxed by the scale of the place and by the sheer guts of what we had done in that "back of beyond" place!'

TIPS TO APPROACH A RETAILER

1. Think Big, Start Small – Finding the Right Fit

While it may be tempting to reach out to the biggest store you can find to make your pitch, it's important to temper your expectations. Finding the right fit is all about where you are right now in your design career. Have you already been in a national-level fashion show, have stylists used your designs for magazine shoots, and do you have thousands of satisfied customers? If so you should be getting out of your living room or the boutique down the road and setting your sights higher. However, if all you have is a portfolio of designs, hold on. Start small, but think big. First of all, find a few clients. As you grow, try and get your clothes sold at smaller boutiques and other stores, and find innovative ways to sell your designs, such as local exhibitions, social media and online stores.

2. Finding the Right Contact

Every store, whether it's that independent boutique around the corner or the big department store in the city's biggest mall, has somebody or a team of 'somebodies' doing the 'buying' for them. Globally, the people who take the call on what is stocked at the shop are called buyers or merchandisers. (However, while researching this book, I called a big, multi-brand department store and was informed that they had no buyers. Perhaps they are not called buyers or merchandisers at a particular store. The point is to find the person or the team of people that buy for that particular store.)

As I discovered during the research for this book, the process is not as transparent as it perhaps is in countries with more established retail buying processes, such as the US. However, there is definitely somebody doing the buying. Finding the right contact is half the job done. How can you find the right contact? It depends on the size of the business you intend to approach. If it's a small local boutique, you may want to simply walk in and ask what time the owner will be around. There's absolutely no harm walking in with a few samples, cut-outs of media publicity or coverage and/or portfolio of your designs. However, if you're targeting a bigger store, the best way to do it is through the web. Look for the corporate site of a brand. Most retailers have e-commerce sites so a general search can take you there. The corporate site is more about the business, the vision, and the people who work there.

EXPLORE!

Look through these links www.mywestside.com (Google 'Westside + Trend India'), www.pantaloons.com (Google 'Pantaloons + India') and www.corporate.shoppersstop. com (Google 'shoppers stop + corporate'). Can you find the contact details of the corporate office? Similarly, you may want to look through sites of Kimaya India and the Facebook Page of Ffolio Bangalore (Google 'Kimaya' + 'designer' + 'India' and 'Ffoliobangalore Facebook'). Some stores such as Ffolio may not have a website and you can always get their details from their Facebook or Google pages.

---

3. Making Your Presentation

Here is what you will need to make your presentation to retailers.

Portfolio: While this is not exactly a 'how to fashion design' book, I do have an interesting first chapter with ideas on how to make a good portfolio. Look through Chapter 1 for ideas and work on a good portfolio of designs.

Samples: We've discussed finding a good master tailor as a first step to bringing your designs to life. Many designers have shared stories of how they started off with one or two tailors who were also great at making patterns and cutting. Find your first employee, get your samples made. Also look through Chapter 4, which has more information on manufacturing.

Business Records: As soon as your business gets profitable, get an accountant to do your bookkeeping for you. An official record of your business profits will help retailers understand that your designs are popular among clients and are making profits for you, and can do the same for them.

4. Means to Deliver

Depending on the order the retailer may be considering to give you, you may be asked how you intend to deliver, if you can deliver on time, if you have the means to do so, etc. Placing an order and not receiving it means the space allotted to your brand remains vacant or, worse, your order may be cancelled. You may need a mini-business plan in place to help you cope with a potential order. Your presentation to the retailer may also have to demonstrate that you have the money and the resources to cope with a big order. Chapter 2 of this book deals with creating a business plan for a new or existing small business. You may borrow a few ideas from here for your presentation.

Also, remember how formal the presentation to the retailer is going to be depends entirely on the size of the retailer, your brand and other factors. Showing up at a small boutique with a business plan for five extra orders every month isn't really necessary!

SETTING UP YOUR OWN BRICKS AND MORTAR STORE

Some designers have a loyal clientele and a large enough customer base to sustain a stand-alone store. Other designers may not be able to get a good enough deal from a large retailer and may decide that running a successful store is the first step to retail growth. Whatever the reason, as long as you're confident that your own boutique can be financially viable in the medium-to-long run, you can set up your own store. Also, take into account the fact that stores have to be managed by good managers, leaving enough time for you to continue designing.

Location, Location, Location

Finding the right space for your store is an important strategic decision. You can't set up a shop in a secluded part of the city. You will not have enough footfalls (people walking into the shop) and that may even dissuade your loyal customers. On the other hand, stores that are likely to have frequent visitors such as those located in a popular mall or a location in the centre of the city may have higher rents. You have to discuss with your accountant or manager and decide how much you can spare every month for your own stand-alone store.

Also keep in mind that commercial real-estate rents are much higher. You may find that a few hundred square feet in a good location costs more than a swanky apartment in the city you live in. However, finding the right location can also pay off huge dividends. You may gain many new customers, develop a larger customer base and grow enough to set up another store. It is a high risk-high reward move and designers confident of their products often do it.

Stocking Right

Before and after you do find the right spot for your store, you may want to ensure that you're performing at your creative and productive best. When you launch your store, you may want to have a little launch party, invite friends, family, media and, if possible, a few local celebrities. You will want to have the absolute best on display. Also, to ensure that walk-ins get converted to customers and then repeat customers, the quality of your designs and products will have to be high. If you find a good location and your work is good, there is no reason why your business shouldn't grow (provided, of course, other factors support you, such as a healthy economic environment and good demand).

OTHER OPTIONS TO SELL YOUR CLOTHES

While the market is structured in a way that designates specific places for commercial activity, as an upcoming designer you can think beyond the brick-and-mortar retail box (and also online shops, which we will be discussing in more detail below). Here are a few ideas to get you going. Go through these suggestions and list a few ideas of your own in your fashion sketchbook.

Exhibitions

Local exhibitions are a great way for designers to sell their clothes and make a little profit. Exhibition halls in cities are available for rent. Many halls will have lean periods when their spaces are not in demand. You can book them at a cheaper rate during that time. Exhibitions are also a great low-risk way of testing the market or your pricing strategy. 'My first big sale happened at an exhibition. When the clothes just disappeared on the first day, I realized I was pricing my clothes too low,' says Chandigarh-based designer Sohni Makkar.

Home Boutiques

Often the exorbitant retail rents make designers sell their clothes from home. Please check if your apartment association or local laws permit commercial activity. That said, residential and commercial zone laws are rarely implemented in India. You can publicize your home boutique at local clubs, apartment building notices, social media, etc.

Cafés and Bookstores

Explore the fun and creative spaces in your locality or city run by supportive entrepreneurs. Perhaps, they may let you display your collection on certain days of the week. In return for sharing their space with you, they may get a lot more people visiting their café or store. This can be a particularly exciting option for a new designer with a handful of clients. Just getting your collection in a public place can be the motivation you need.

EXPLORE!

In the retail business, this kind of selling is called 'Shop-in-Shop'. Google 'Shop-in-Shop' + India for information on how the retail selling format is catching on in India. You should find many news articles on this. (Be sure to use the phrase Shop-in-Shop with double quotes as show 'Shop-in-Shop' for best results)

Commercial Place with Space or the Pop-up Store!

If your business is doing relatively well but is yet not big enough for a full-fledged retail space, you may want to explore different kinds of commercial areas that may be available for rent – say, a smaller area in a big retail store selling accessories, or a little space in a big salon, or in the public areas of a mall, etc. Get creative and you can make a little money go a long way.

Spaces that are rented for a short term in a privately owned commercial space such as a mall (or just about anywhere where customers can find you) are called pop-up stores. These kinds of stores have been around in all the cool cities you can think of – London, New York, Hong Kong, Singapore, Paris, etc., – since the '90s. One of the reasons is the lack of space in these cities that make rents super expensive. Designers and labels of all sizes, therefore, hire small spaces for rent on a temporary basis. This could be anywhere from two to three months, and the space could be as tiny as 200 sq. ft.

The pop-up store has also gained popularity in India. It is often associated with cool and edgy stores with spaces to offer for rent and fun brands. The hip hangout spot in Delhi, One Style Mile, the quirky Bungalow 8 store in Colaba and Maison Boutique in Bangalore, have hosted regular and store-in-store pop-ups over the last few years. Many international brands are also testing the marketing with pop-up stores. Rather than have a big launch and invest in a huge retail space, they choose to hire a small space in a mall or some place with enough footfalls and see how things go. Isn't that a great idea for a cash-strapped entrepreneur as well?

DO IT!

Can you make a list of funky cafés or cool shops owned by independent entrepreneurs in your city? Do you think they'd be open to the idea of having a pop-up store for your brand? The location you choose for the pop-up store will also depend on the kinds of clothes you design. What are the spaces that are ideal for your designs?

SELLING YOUR CLOTHES ONLINE

E-commerce has revolutionized the way business is done in India (and around the world, of course). The online shopping bug has bitten Indian customers a little later than it did in other parts of the world but, boy, have we taken to it! So what does the growing rate of Internet shopping do for entrepreneurs like you?

First of all, online retail 'space' is cheap. As designer Anita Dongre says, 'Today, there are ample opportunities for young designers to set shop. If you do not have the required resources to set up a store, go online. E-commerce is looking at fashion as a big business opportunity. Social media platforms too, like Facebook, enable you to connect with your audience, and take orders online. Better still, create your own e-store!'

You may have to pay anywhere from Rs 50,000 to several lakhs for retail space in a prime location of a big city, while registering a domain name is very cheap. Even setting up an online store can be done in a few thousand rupees! Not only is it a cheap alternative, online retail is also a great opportunity and a crucial one for upcoming fashion entrepreneurs to seize!

Pernia Qureshi is a designer and stylist who set up Pernia's pop-up shop (www.perniaspopupshop.com), an online fashion store that curates and sells some of the finest Indian designer wear. 'Online platforms are very important for young and upcoming designers. In today's world, everyone is on some social media platform or other. Everything now is just a click away. This is what gives an advantage to those upcoming designers who lack experience. They can always sell their stuff online to see how their product sells before actually investing or renting a space to sell what they make,' says Pernia.

Designer Sekuzo Sovenyi, who has been featured in the earlier chapters, has been retailing exclusively on his Facebook page over the last year. Fashion e-commerce stores like koovs. com and donebynone.com are also retail brands that have been created to be sold exclusively online.

IDEAS ON HOW TO SELL YOUR CLOTHES ON THE INTERNET

1. Selling Through an Existing E-Commerce Site

The sheer number of online fashion sites and websites that also sell apparel and accessories has opened up the market for young designers. Some very popular sites like Myntra and Jabong sell brands that are also widely available online, while other sites like Donebynone (donebynone.com) sell clothes exclusively designed for online consumers. Exclusive designer stores like Pernia's Pop-up sell a host of established designers and also introduce talented new designers almost every week.

Pernia shares how designers get a chance to be sold on her popular site. 'We're always willing to introduce new and upcoming designers on our website. We mainly look for designers who are willing to experiment and take designing to a whole new level. Someone who's got a different yet stylish approach to Indian fashion and is willing to give their best to Pernia's pop-up shop,' she explains.

The first step, of course, as Pernia says, is to have great designs. However, getting featured and sold on these sites needs more work. Here are a few steps you could follow.

- Shortlist a bunch of sites that are a good fit for your style. Look at what the sites sell. If they sell couture and you design work-out clothes, it's a total mismatch. Always target the right websites.
- Find the right contact. Pick up the phone and call them if their number is listed on the site. Ask for the email of the buyer/merchandiser and tell them you'd like to send your portfolio. If you don't get a response in the first call, keep trying. (Know when to move on though!)
- Prepare a nice portfolio that includes your designs, photographs, media coverage, if any, client profile and other important information that may convince the website that you will make profits for them – such as great sales or celebrity fans, or even a huge number of Facebook fans! If you can't do this yourself, hire a freelance writer or PR professional to do this for you.

EXPLORE!

Make a list of websites that sell clothes online. Find as many as you can, or up to a certain number such as fifty. Out of this list, make a list of ten sites that you really love and would love to see your designs sold on. Start with the following Google terms 'online fashion store + India'.

2. Use Social Media for Sales

I covered the importance of social media for fashion designers in Chapter 5, where I spoke about the importance of these tools for marketing. However, many entrepreneurs are using social media to sell their products on a much smaller scale. Some of them view it as a first step to selling their products on a larger e-commerce platform.

If you already have Facebook, Instagram, Pinterest and other accounts for your brand, you may want to consider setting up separate pages exclusively to sell your products. Of course, you will have to take a call on whether you need double accounts depending on how extensively you use social media for marketing.

You could use the albums and picture upload options on the various social media sites to create a beautiful visual product catalogue. On Facebook you can create several albums which gives you the advantage of separating products by month of launch or other innovative titles such as 'Sold', 'New Arrivals', etc. Your buyers could also leave comments in the user section, which works as the 'Review' section of an e-commerce site.

You can take orders and receive payments in an informal way, where potential buyers send you enquiries on e-mail, post demand drafts or do bank transfer. However, depending on how many customers you get on social media, you must absolutely try the various Facebook e-commerce application options. These applications give your visitors a 'Buy' option and integrates a payment gateway (means to pay with debit or credit cards) into your page.

EXPLORE!

If you're shopping for a Facebook e-commerce application, explore these options: Payvment, ShopTab and Voiyk (Google the words). But remember that new e-commerce applications are launched frequently. Use these suggestions as a starting point. Explore the new applications, compare and install the one that best suits your needs. Most of the applications do require a fee, however, many of them offer free trial periods. So you can absolutely try more than one and see if it works for you.

If you're an avid blogger and use any of the popular blogging platforms such as Wordpress or Blogger, you can also take orders through those sites. If you have many readers and followers, you could get them to support you by buying your products right from your blog without redirecting them anywhere else. Several e-commerce platforms have been developed for this purpose and you can easily find one that works for you. Even if you don't have a blog but are serious about selling online through your own space, you can use this as the first step to setting up a full-fledged e-commerce site.

3. Set Up an E-Commerce Site

The success of home-grown online stores such as Flipkart and Snapdeal has finally made Indian industry wake up to the potential of e-commerce. The enthusiasm for e-commerce has trickled all the way down to the independent entrepreneur. Many upcoming and established designers are setting up their own online retail spaces to reach out to the savvy online customer.

More importantly, no matter where you're based in India, whether in New Delhi or Nagpur, and irrespective of the size of your business, if you have the talent, you can get yourself noticed by simply setting up an e-commerce site.

As Pernia Qureshi says, 'Through online retail space and media, an aspiring designer can build for himself a strong platform to sell his product. Even if he/she lives in the most secluded area, he/she will always be connected to his target audience through an online space. So when it comes to selling things online, nobody's at a disadvantage.'

Did we just say 'simply' set up? Yes, if you haven't explored this option yet, setting up an e-commerce site is not as complicated as you may think it is. We mentioned the use of e-commerce applications for social media sites in the earlier section. Setting up a full-fledged, independent online store is almost as simple as that. You will need to start by finding the right e-commerce platform to suit your business.

Some of the popular e-commerce platforms for small business owners are: Zepo (www.zepo.in), Shopify (www.shopify.in) and Magento (Magento.com). Zepo and Shopify are home-grown e-commerce platforms and have lots of India-based entrepreneurs who've shared their testimonials on these sites.

You will also find links to some fashion and accessories-based businesses on these sites. Magento is an ebay-owned business and you will find many international testimonials, mainly by American entrepreneurs. However, Magento is popular among Indian entrepreneurs as well.

As always, do remember that new e-commerce platforms are created and launched often. Do remember to explore options other than the ones mentioned here. You can use them as starting points for your search. Several blogs and sites review e-commerce platforms and that may be a good way to get other recommendations too.

Most of these platforms are user-friendly and, if needed, you may have to hire a freelancer to help you with minor tweaks. An additional support person can't hurt a small business too much. After you've chosen a platform for your e-store, you will have to upload photographs of your designs and create product catalogues. Once that is done, you're on your way to running your own online store!

9

YOUR FIRST FASHION WEEK

The fashion industry is full of terminology and jargon. Beyond the art of designing, fashion is a precision science. Ever tried stitching a garment? (Which is why we've recommended sewing classes at every possible opportunity in this book!) You have to get exactly the right cut, the perfect measurements, the best possible fit, etc. That's when well-designed clothes look gorgeous.

Further, fashion is big business. This means customer demographics, analytics, marketing and other factors are also incredibly important. Most of it is common sense and if you have a knack for business, you will understand them all as you go along. In this book, I've discussed several important areas of fashion entrepreneurship and also demystified a lot of jargon. However, one important area remains – fashion seasons!

Fashion seasons drive the entire fashion industry. Every year, the whole world of fashion rushes to meet deadlines and targets for two or three of the major fashion seasons.

WHAT IS A FASHION SEASON?

Not all of us understand fashion seasons well. (And apologies in advance if you're hooked to fashion weeks that happen all around the world and can tell Spring/Summer from Holiday/Resort!) But fashion seasons are a relatively new concept in India, so you may be an aspiring designer or already have a small fashion business but not know a thing about fashion seasons. Also, most fashion entrepreneurs across the country design by instinct. For instance, the wedding season in north India means designers try to get their slice of the pie by designing couture or blingy accessories or even festive pret!

Generally speaking, retailers follow their own annual calendar called the 'retail year'. In countries in the Northern Hemisphere, which includes the US, the UK and France, Spring/Summer collections are launched in February and are sold all the way up to June. Clothes designed specifically for Fall/Winter are sold in stores from August to December. In countries in the Southern Hemisphere, including Australia, South Africa and New Zealand, fashion seasons are different because seasons are different. So, for instance, in Australia, summer collections are showcased in May.

In many parts of the world, including some parts of the Northern Hemisphere that enjoy year-round warm weather, Summer/Resort, Holiday/Resort, Spring/Festive and Winter/Festive are also popular retail seasons.

In India, fashion shows and retailers largely sell Summer/Resort and Fashion/Festive. In retail markets in northern India, winter collections are also big business.

Jargon Out

If all this sounds complicated and intimidating, don't fret. If you're just starting out as a designer and catering to regional markets, go by your instinct. Design for the local season. You will see it all around you!

DO IT!

Here's an exciting project idea for you. In your fashion sketchbook or journal, make a list of seasons you've read here, from Spring/Summer to Summer/Festive. Find images on Google with key phrases like 'Spring/Summer <year of your choice>'. Download and get them printed on nice, glossy paper. Stick the pictures under the corresponding season. There! You have yourself a nice, personalized visual guide to various fashion seasons. Of course, feel free to adapt this project as convenient to you. Can't get glossy paper? Just get it on regular paper. Want to make a PDF instead of getting it in your fashion sketchbook? Sure. Have fun and learn at the same time.

WHAT ARE FASHION WEEKS?

A fashion week is a series of fashion shows put together by designers and fashion labels. Why is it a week? Because of history. Seriously. Americans first ran a series of fashion shows in New York, inviting members of the industry and the press, calling it the Press Week. This was in 1943. When the Press Week became a grand success, other countries adapted the concept of 'weekly' fashion shows, where the latest designs and collections were shown.

If you remember your history lessons, World War II happened from 1939 to 1945. The war was mostly concentrated in Europe. This means in 1943, when Americans were holding the first 'Fashion Week', Europe was in the middle of war. For a long time European countries such as France and Italy were the cornerstones of fashion. However, after the long war, their economies were devastated and recovered very slowly.

Therefore, the first fashion week that took place in Europe, specifically in Paris, took place only in 1973. About fifty years later, four major global fashion weeks have emerged – three of them from Europe. These are major international events and the goings-on at these fashion weeks are covered by the press in almost every major country in the world, including in India.

The 'Big Four' fashion weeks are the Paris Fashion Week, London Fashion Week, New York Fashion Week and Milan Fashion Week. I will talk a little more about them but here's an important question that you should be asking: Why should I know about fashion weeks?

As a designer you get a sense of where the industry is going, what the latest collections are all about, what established designers are up to and more. However, fashion weeks are more than that. The fashion week is also an incredibly important trade event. (Okay, now what the hell is a trade event, right?)

Trade Events/Shows

Bear with us here. This is a brief but crucial explanation that will help you understand Fashion Weeks a little bit more. Trade Events or Trade Shows or Trade Exhibitions are events specific to a particular industry where the latest products or services are displayed or announced. Every industry has major trade shows from time to time. For instance, the mobile phone industry will display its latest phone models with new features at a trade show. Journalists, bloggers, businesses related to the industry (such as mobile phone spare part manufacturers) and others will attend the event.

Similarly, fashion weeks are huge trade events. Buyers (for big and small retail chains or stores), merchandisers, trend scouts, editors, journalists and others attend the event. Much more money than you can imagine is exchanged, many more brands are made and unmade during these events. For instance, a new fashion designer maybe launched at a fashion week and a buyer (I've explained what a buyer does in Chapter 8) may be impressed by this designer and decide to stock his collection at shops across the country. Thus, a newbie fashion designer today can become a household brand name tomorrow! The fashion week is a big business event.

I've discussed in earlier chapters (specifically Chapter 2) that as a fashion entrepreneur you should think both as a creative artist and a business person. The next time you follow a fashion week, try to think not just of how the designs look but also how a particular collection may have influenced the business and the industry.

HOW FASHION WEEKS CAN INFLUENCE YOUR BUSINESS?

No matter how big or small your fashion label is, fashion weeks can have an impact on your business. The following sections tell us why.

Media Hype

The major fashion weeks in India and abroad find rampant coverage by press across the country. Many fashion weeks in India are influenced by the shows abroad. Top designers routinely use Bollywood stars to model clothes for them. This means everybody, including your customer, is attuned to the latest trends and looks of the season. Granted, you may not want to create similar designs and may have your own ideas, but almost every upcoming designer has to cater to customer demand created by the more established designers. If you're tempted to replicate these designs, we strongly advocate you don't (Read Chapter 3 on patent and copyrights). Nonetheless, being aware of the latest 'looks' makes excellent business sense.

Launch Your Label

If you're selected to enter one of the big fashion weeks in India, this could help launch your label on a bigger scale, as showing at one of the fashion weeks means unprecedented exposure and publicity.

And More ...

Going from the new entrant fashion designer category to an established designer category (every big fashion week has these categories) means you're now officially embedded in the fashion industry in India. Sure, a lot of fashion entrepreneurs make a conscious choice to remain working designers. Perhaps they don't want the publicity or the hype, and would prefer to cater to their regional clients. Further, not every designer wants to invest the money and energy into designing clothes that they aren't sure will sell in the immediate 'real market'.

There's nothing wrong with either position and it's up to you to decide to participate or not. Or even postpone that decision until you actually get your business up and running.

WORLD FAMOUS FASHION WEEKS – THE BIG FOUR

Now that you know how important fashion weeks are for the industry and also independent entrepreneurs like you, here's a quick primer on the top fashion weeks from around the world. (Enjoy the fun 'Explore!' activities under each heading!)

New York Fashion Week

American media and culture have been broadcast so widely that most of us to know that New York equals the fashion Mecca. This fashion week kicks off the top four fashion weeks. With the New York event, the 'Fashion Month' (i.e. one major fashion week every week of the month) officially begins travelling to Paris, London and Milan.

EXPLORE!

Look at the other fashion weeks in America, such as 'Miami Fashion Week' and 'San Francisco Fashion Week'. Think of a major city in that country and it has a Fashion Week.

Paris Fashion Week

Paris has always been and will probably continue to be the capital of fashion. In the 19th century, many countries around the world, including America and Russia, took inspiration from Parisian trends. Today, it has stiff competition from the other cities in the 'Big Four' but continues to inspire. With big, Western-oriented fashion markets developing in countries like India and China, the Paris Fashion Week's sphere of influence is set to expand.

The Paris Fashion Week is held twice every year. Designers come together here to show their Spring/Summer or Autumn/Winter collections.

EXPLORE!

Google 'Paris Fashion Week + Top Designers + <your preferred year>' Enjoy what you find. You're likely to also see what looks were in, which designers were popular and how many of them set trends for the following years.

Milan Fashion Week

Gucci, Versace, Armani – what would the world of fashion be without these top Italian designers! Luckily for them, they had a great platform to use as springboard to global fame – the Milan Fashion Week. This fashion week attracts a great deal of global attention and is partly responsible for making so many Italian brands globally famous.

Like the other fashion weeks you've seen so far, this event is also held twice year; showcasing Spring/Summer and Autumn/Winter collections.

EXPLORE!

The Milan Fashion Week has been in the eye of a storm for hiring underage models. Google 'Milan Fashion Week + Models + Age' to know more. What is your take on this as an upcoming fashion designer? What do you think about the clothes they model?

London Fashion Week

As much as American fashion is popular in India (mainly through television and films), Indians remain culturally connected to London in many ways. Till the late '80s, London was the top go-to destination for affluent Indians for shopping and vacations. In recent years, Paris, New York, Milan have taken away some of London's potential Indian fashion shoppers. However, when it comes to India and indeed to the rest of the world, London is still one of the fashion capitals of the world and many trends do indeed emerge from this city. Watch out for the bi-annual London Fashion Week every year.

EXPLORE!

The organizers of London Fashion Week are great at promoting their event on the Internet. The website –

> www.londonfashionweek.co.uk/ – hosts hundreds of videos from the fashion week. Also, you can watch the fashion week live, thanks to live streaming on the website. See, you don't even have to go to London to get inspired!

FAMOUS FASHION WEEKS IN INDIA

Up until 1991, India was a closed economy. This meant that we had very few foreign brands and Indian entrepreneurs had to deal with too many challenges. After the economy opened up to foreign investment, several industries, including fashion, have been transformed.

Designer Anita Dongre says, 'The Indian fashion industry today is definitely more organized than what it was fifteen years ago, and continues to grow at a rapid pace, with a new pool of talent emerging every season ... Over the years, the fashion weeks in India have emerged as the country's premier launching pad for young designers, through many programmes designed to cultivate and promote new talent.'

Our fashion industry felt confident enough to launch its own fashion events. Thus the Lakme India Fashion Week, Wills Lifestyle Fashion Week and others were born. Here are a few facts about some of India's prominent fashion weeks and how you can be a part of them.

Lakme India Fashion Week

Undoubtedly, one of the biggest fashion shows in India! Lakme India Fashion Week was launched in 1999 and receives great publicity year after year. The fashion week is held twice a year – Summer/Resort in February and Winter/Festive in August. For many designers, showcasing their collection at the Lakme India Fashion Week has been the ultimate launch pad.

How to enter? Lakme India Fashion Week has Gen-Next and Emerging Designers' categories for young designers. Several popular designers like Masaba Gupta and Tanya Sharma started their careers in the Gen-Next category. Application forms and all the material required to enter the fashion week is available on the event's official website. Log onto 'Lakmefashionweek. co.in'. Access the 'Registrations' Tab. You will find both the Gen-Next and Emerging Designers category. Submit a full, well-made application and wait to be invited. If you fail the first year, don't fret. Keep trying!

Please note that websites are frequently updated or changed, so if you don't find the registrations' tab mentioned here, simply Google the following: 'Lakme Fashion Week + Gen-Next + Registrations'.

Amazon India Fashion Week (Formerly known as Wills Lifestyle India Fashion Week)

This started off as India Fashion Week, just a year after Lakme India Fashion Week, in 2000. The launch of the Wills Lifestyle India Fashion Week created a split in the fashion industry in the earlier years. However, in recent times, the Indian fashion industry in general has been functioning in a coherent manner.

This event is held in Delhi, again, twice a year. However, the fashion calendar followed by the Amazon India Fashion Week is different from the Lakme Indian Fashion Week. This event is scheduled to showcase Autumn/Winter collections in March and Spring/Summer collections in October. Many prominent designers such as Sabyasachi Mukherjee have debuted at the India Fashion Week.

How to enter? Amazon India Fashion Week is very closely connected to the Fashion Design Council of India (FDCI). To enter the fashion week, you have to first secure membership at FDCI. As a member you will be able to apply to register for the fashion week. On selection, you can take your collection to Delhi!

Log onto www.fdci.org. Look in the FAQs section on entering events, which includes the fashion week. If for whatever reason you fail to find this information (website change, etc.), you can always call the numbers listed on the site.

DO IT!

In addition to organizing fashion events like the fashion week, FDCI aims to help upcoming designers with other resources such as training and counselling. Be sure to subscribe to their newsletter to stay abreast of the latest in the industry and also get information about the possible resources that you could benefit from. You should be able to find the 'Newsletter' tab on the home page. Here's the link again: www.fdci.org

---

Blender's Pride Bangalore Fashion Week

In recent years, Bangalore Fashion Week has also gained prominence. Some industry experts have forecast a split of the fashion scene across three zones – North (Wills Lifestyle Fashion Week), West (Lakme India Fashion Week) and South (Blender's Pride Bangalore Fashion Week). However, the fashion week scenario is still evolving and there are many contenders. So stay tuned and make your own list of top fashion weeks in India.

How to enter? Simple enough. Log onto www. bangalorefashionweek.in. Find the 'Registrations' link and register. The categories are identical to the Lakme Fashion Week. 'Gen-next' for newbies and 'Emerging designers' for those who've been around longer.

How to Maximize Chances of Getting into Fashion Weeks?

Run a Fashion Label: The major fashion weeks mentioned here require that entrants have at least a few years' experience in designing for their own label. So even before you think of showcasing your collection at one of these events you need to start your journey as a fashion entrepreneur first.

Good Work: Since the fashion industry was in its nascent stages in the last decade, eligibility and selection criteria were not that stringent. However, in the forthcoming years, competition to showcase at the best fashion weeks is set to get intense. The better your work, the better your chances of getting in.

A Profitable Business: A steadily growing business with loyal customers can only help you, whether you're looking to enter a fashion week or seeking a loan from a bank!

Media Publicity: Popularity in the media is helpful, perhaps, even more so than profits (at least as far as entering fashion weeks are concerned). Fashion Weeks are events that make money for the organizers as well, therefore, designers that create a buzz in the media are always welcome. Giving your clothes for photo shoots, reaching out to fashion journalists and bloggers from time to time is always a good idea if you're aiming to showcase your collection at one of these events.

Budgeting Your Fashion Week Entry

Clothes: Fashion week shows display hundreds of outfits from each designer. You will have to have the budget to create enough clothes.

Models: Depending on your budget and collection, you will have to contract models for your showcase.

Stylists and Make-up Artists: Very important for any fashion show.

Design Assistants: If you've been running a small label with very few employees, this is the time you may want to consider hiring an assistant.

Caution

With so many new fashion weeks and events being launched across the country, you will have to take into consideration various factors before showcasing your collection. Given the time and money required for a single exhibit of this kind, you must find out if the organizers are reputable, if the event has been around for a certain number of years, if it really garners that kind of publicity you're looking for, and more.

Internationally, designers go to great lengths to show at the fashion week, even going into debt for it. But they know that exposure at one of the 'Big Four' fashion weeks can mean fame and fortune. That is not necessarily true for all fashion weeks, and definitely not true for many of the fashion weeks run by fly-by-night event organizers in India. You may want to wait to get into the best fashion week before showing your collection or take a chance and show at a smaller but reputed show as a first step.

INSPIRATION — TANYA SHARMA, CHAITANYA RAO AND EINA AHLUWALIA

Read about how the designers interviewed for this book were chosen to show at the Lakme India Fashion week, the lessons they learnt, how fashion weeks have helped their label and more!

TANYA SHARMA (GAGA STUDIO), MUMBAI

'After graduating from NIFT, Mumbai, I started with small collections that were sold in local boutiques. I tested my label Gaga and it seemed to be doing well, so I decided to give it a push. To take it further, I applied to show at the Lakme India Fashion Week in the 'Gen-Next' category, which is for new designers.

That was the starting point for my label. After that I did three more seasons, showcasing my collection at the Lakme India Fashion Week. Things took off and now my collection is shown at the fashion week in the established designers' category! Trying to do something new every season and showcasing at the fashion week helped take my label forward.'

CHAITANYA RAO (EPONYMOUS LABEL), CHENNAI

'I started my label in the '90s, so I took some time to showcase my collection at the fashion week. My clothes were retailing, I was designing and styling celebrities and actors for films, ad commercials, etc. My label was being recognized. I thought to myself, "What next?" At this point, I felt that I must showcase at the fashion week. I registered for the Lakme India Fashion Week in 2007 and I got through. I showcased my collection and then there's the pressure to constantly showcase your work every season, or at least every year. Of course, you get a lot of editorial coverage and publicity and that's a great thing. But then, one also has to be ready to supply to the market as the demand for your products does go up. I would make the mistake of showcasing my collection and then I would get busy with my other work such as designing for films and so on. That's something I've learnt from my experience at fashion weeks.'

EINA AHLUWALIA (EPONYMOUS LABEL), KOLKATA

'I launched my own jewellery and accessories label in 2002. After several years of running my own label successfully, I was still hesitant to apply to the fashion week. I thought, "Why would they choose us?" and I was so wrong. I was selected to show at the Lakme India Fashion Week. So I would absolutely encourage young designers to try. Since 2009, I have been showcasing my collection at fashion weeks and other shows and love the response I get.'

10

KEEP GOING!
STAYING MOTIVATED IN THE SHORT-,
MEDIUM- AND LONG-TERM

As your business takes off, you will find that each passing year comes with its own set of unique challenges. While there are a few 'serial' entrepreneurs who hop from one business to another, others will want their businesses to stand the test of time. This is particularly true of the fashion business – because a legacy is not built in a day. In fact, fashion entrepreneurs nurture their business with such furious, consistent passion, for decades at a stretch, that their work is more recognizable than their personal identity. What do you think of when you hear Dolce & Gabbana? The D&G logo or the two Italian designers?

So when I urge you to 'Keep Going', I foresee a long, fruitful journey for you. But here's the catch – staying motivated all the way through is not easy. The sensible thing to do for any goal that transcends several decades is, as the cliché goes, to divide it into easy achievable targets. Here I'll tell you about some of the specific challenges of each phase – short, medium and long-term and show you how you can keep going.

But before that, a little note on that dreaded 'M' word, motivation. There are days when it can seem like you've never had it, and are in for a long, uneventful life because you can't get yourself out of bed! It happens to the best of us, which is why there are hundreds of books on the subject, so many psychologists dedicating their lives to 'motivation' research, and thousands of blogs and websites based on the topic. This means, there are enough resources for you to give yourself a little pep when you need it the most.

Here's one for you to start with.

EXPLORE!

Career Analyst Dan Pink's TED Talk 'The Puzzle of Motivation' (subtitled in forty-two languages) has inspired millions of people around the world, since the first time it was released in 2009. To watch the video, Google 'Dan Pink + Motivation + TED Talk'.

KEEP GOING: YEAR ONE TO FIVE

Most fashion entrepreneurs we spoke to said starting a business was the easiest thing, so these first few years shouldn't be difficult for you. And yet, this is the period within which most businesses shut down for a whole host of reasons. 'Most people get into the fashion business, because it's exciting, but after the first few years, only those with the real passion for it are able to stay in the market,' says Tanya Sharma of Gaga, who has had her own label for over five years now.

Keep Going Mantra: Enjoy the Little Things

In the first few years, there may be difficult moments – you may not make as much money, you may have to change your strategy many times, or you may find your business has taken off so much that you feel out of control. So from year one to five, we suggest you enjoy the little things. Being your own boss means you keep your own timings and live life your own way. When Eina Ahluwalia quit her cushy job in management to start her own jewellery designing business, it was the little things that kept her going and not wanting to ever get back to a job.

'When I quit my job and started designing jewellery, I was definitely doing something I loved but it also gave me the flexibility to work at my own pace and in my own time. I could work at three in the morning or three in the afternoon. It was up to me and I loved it,' she says.

Enjoying the little things also means celebrating the successes which may not seem so big at that time but contribute to your long-term success, such as getting a new customer, reading a positive review or simply designing something you love.

KEEP GOING: YEAR SIX TO TEN

During this time, things could get pretty intense. You're probably well-known in the region by now, and if you're lucky, across the nation. Competition is fierce in this category, and there are many designers and fashion businesses vying for the attention of your clients. This is the time to stand out, stay consistently motivated and be continuously creative, so you can build and grow the name you've created for yourself. But how?

Keep Going Mantra: Focus On All Things Important

'If I honed in on how much money I am making, and turned it into some sort of a benchmark for success, I would go crazy. Having been in this business for so many years, I have realized that money comes and goes, and I need something more valuable, more worthy of my attention,' says Tanya Sharma.

So what keeps her going? Three words: the work, the work, the work. 'At this point, I work to produce better and better designs and that is what makes it a delight to still have a business while many others who may have been around a few years ago have just faded away,' she says.

Focusing on the work keeps you excited, and when you're excited about your work, you hardly need to motivate yourself. Right? Okay, maybe you need to push yourself a little but not as much as if you were focused on things that you didn't value as much. Having caught the eye of major Bollywood stars, perhaps Tanya Sharma isn't so far off the mark after all.

KEEP GOING: ELEVEN YEARS AND BEYOND

If you've been around for this long, there's hardly a reason for you to stop. Your focus at this point will have to be on expanding your existing business and taking your business to greater heights and perhaps, even trying something new.

After over two decades as a designer, entrepreneur and 'Couture King', JJ Valaya continues to explore. When we interviewed him for this book, he was busy with his latest pet-project Valaya Homes, where his design sensibility meets interior decoration. But what is it that really keeps a fashion entrepreneur going after a decade in the business?

Keep Going Mantra: Seek and Find Meaning

'There are months when you work really hard,' says Eina. 'I have worked fourteen to sixteen hours, but then, if you love learning and enjoy what you're doing, you will keep at it, even after so many years,' she says, having launched her jewellery brand over twelve years ago.

But most importantly, Eina's unwavering motivation comes from a quest for meaning. Thinking of her life before she started her business, she says, 'It's not that I hated my job, but I felt like I wasn't doing anything meaningful. At this point, there is real meaning in what I am doing. My question is always: How am I making my own life meaningful? How am I adding value to somebody else's life?' One just has to take a look at Eina's work, and the awards and accolades she's won in the last few years to know she practises what she says. So why not take her words as an inspiration to keep you going when you need it the most! .

Appendix

All the helpful tips published under the various headers are curated in this section for you.

CHAPTER 1 – BECOME A MASTER OF FASHION DESIGN

Do it!

You may choose to start a 'scrapbook' (a book where you put together scraps or pieces of information, pictures, etc.) In your book, start to collect information, note down tips and practise your drawing skills. Several experts, amateurs and students share tricks and tips related to the art of fashion illustration on YouTube and various blogs. Jot down relevant ideas in your scrapbook. Pinterest is another site that can give you a great deal of visual exposure to this art form. Take printouts of illustrations you like and post them in your book. You can also go to Amazon.in and find several fashion illustrations books published by famous fashion designers. Use the 'Look Inside' option on Amazon.in to read portions of the book for free!

Explore!

Nicole Kidman, Julia Roberts, Natalie Portman are just a few of the fans of New York-based fashion designer Isaac Mizrahi's designs. Mizrahi's career as a fashion entrepreneur has had many ups and downs. But one thing nobody questions is the designer's creative genius.Check out Isaac Mizrahi's talk on creativity, on the TED Talks website. Many budding fashion designers have found it inspiring. Google: 'Isaac Mizrahi' + 'TED Talks'.

Explore!

With over a lakh views on YouTube, user xxxhey2's thirty minute video on 'Example Art Portfolio for Entry into Fashion Design Degree' has to be the most watched YouTube video on the subject of creating a fashion journal. Log onto YouTube and search 'xxxhey2 + fashion sketchbook'. When you click to watch the video, you will also find related videos on fashion sketchbooks on the right-hand tab. Also, read the comments and discussion under the videos on the subject for more information and better understanding.

Do it!

Buy a simple blank sheet book. In the first three pages, note down quotes that you find inspiring as a fashion designer. In the next three pages, paste magazine cuttings or printouts of your favourite designer outfits. In the next three pages, paste images, quotes or notes on a non-fashion source of inspiration – it could be related to your favourite book, TV show, hobby such as travelling ... absolutely anything that you find inspiring as a designer but with no direct connection to fashion.

There, we've started you off on your first fashion journal!

Explore!

On last count, Amazon.in had close to 300 books on putting together a fashion portfolio. On the homepage, go to the search box, select 'books' instead of 'all' and type 'fashion portfolio'. You will get your results, many of which will have the 'Look Inside' option. This lets you see a few chapters from the book without having to buy it. Enjoy a free preview of books and get more helpful tips on creating your portfolio!

CHAPTER 2 – YOUR FIRST BUSINESS PLAN

Do it!

So you have to create your business plan. If you're not a good writer or just too intimidated to write so much, how about recording your business plan? Most phones these days come with a video/audio record option. So just do it! No excuses. Also, did you know you can write your business plan in any language you choose? Hindi, Kannada or Kashmiri. Absolutely! If ever you need to present your plan to investors or others, simply get it translated for a small fee.

Explore!

Google mission and vision statements of famous fashion companies you admire. For example: Chanel's mission statement is 'To be the Ultimate House of Luxury, defining style and creating desire, now and forever.' Can you find mission or vision statements for five famous fashion houses?

Explore!

To understand more about where the fashion industry in India is today and the direction in which it is headed, Google 'Fashion Industry India' + 'Business Today' or other publicatins of your choice such as 'HT Mint', 'Economic Times', etc.

Explore!

Do you have a family member or a friend with an MBA degree and is somebody you respect? Try and understand each of the components of Section 4.0 of the Business Plan – Marketing Strategy, Pricing Strategy and Sales Strategy. These strategic concepts are very important to understand. Understand the relevance of these sections, independent of the fashion industry. Try to understand what they mean, in general, in the business world.

Explore!

Have you ever seen TV shows that are centred on wannabe entrepreneurs presenting their business plans to venture capitalists? No? Well there are tons of international (mostly American shows) of this nature, the business version of *American Idol*, with singing talent swapped for business acumen. Look them up. For instance, CNBC TV 18 in India has been running a show called 'Start-up Indian Funding Challenge' where entrepreneurs present their ideas. Run search 'Start-up Indian Funding Challenge' on www.youtube.co.in. This will help you understand better how business plans are presented and evaluated.

Do it!

After catching a couple of videos or even episodes of TV shows where entrepreneurs present their ideas to venture capitalists why don't you invite a friend or a family member with experience as an entrepreneur or running a business and present your business plan as though you're looking to be funded? Not only will this get you an informed perspective but you will also feel more objective about your business plan after presenting it. You will find points you feel strongly about and understand areas that you felt didn't sound convincing. Try it. You will have fun!

CHAPTER 4 – DESIGN

Do it!

Think of a theme for a collection. Don't worry about having the perfect theme. It can be absolutely anything. Create a concept board for it, based on the example and explanation given above.

Explore!

Go to www.pinterest.com, in the search box on the home page, key in: 'creative mood boards fashion'. You will find lots of inspiration on concept boards!

Explore!

Log onto a website that sells a wide range of books such as Amazon.co.in and search in the books on brainstorming. Read free previews of as many books that interest you on the subject. You may find fun brainstorming activities, exercises and more. Obviously, if you find any of the books interesting, get them!

Do it!

Visual stimulation time. Use the Google Images tool (go to google.co.in and click the 'images' link. Type in 'mind-mapping fashion design'. Find samples of mind maps. Based on what you find, try and create your own mind map of an idea or theme you've been thinking about for a fashion line.

Explore!

Almost every state in India has its traditional handloom and textiles. Use the Internet to make a list of traditional textiles and handlooms. Aim to put together a list of at least twenty. Google terms: <Name of the state> + Textile + Handloom. Name of the state can be Karnataka, Kerala, Himachal Pradesh, etc.

Do it!

A swatch book is a collection of swatches or fabric samples. Can you create a swatch-book of the list of textiles that you've made? You can source these when you travel or when handloom exhibitions come to your city. You can request friends and relatives to send you these textiles. Find a way to get as many fabric samples as you can. Designer Tanya Sharma suggests that young designers do a course in textiles, these activities are as close as you can get to expanding your knowledge bank on textiles and fabrics while running your fashion business!

Explore!

Go to YouTube.com and search for 'pattern-making class'. This will lead you to several videos that will actually show you how to make patterns and what a pattern-maker does. From the comfort of your home, you can actually get a sense of attending a session in a Fashion school. Because pattern-making is such a visual process, you will need the help of videos to understand it better. Watch as many as you can. Enjoy, learn and grow!

Do it!

This is strictly for novices. Google 'simple free sewing patterns'. You will find hundreds of patterns for various designs. Find one you like and cut out your first pattern in an old newspaper. The next step would be to create a sewing pattern for one of your own designs. Feel ready to do that?

CHAPTER 5 – MARKETING, BRANDING AND MORE

Explore!

Google 'top fashion campaigns' and see what shows up.

Explore!

Check out Anita Dongre's online presence. AND's online marketing team is hard at work ensuring the brand is visible on multiple platforms. Explore the work they do and get inspired. Google: 'Anita Dongre + Facebook or + Instagram'. 'Anita Dongre + Pinterest'. What is Anita's social media strategy? How does it tie in with her brand values and larger marketing strategy?

CHAPTER 6 – YOUR BIG BRAND FASHION LABEL

Explore!

Google 'Industrial Revolution + Fashion' to know more about how industrialization shaped the fashion industry as we know it today, from designing to production to distribution. Don't feel like reading? Search 'industrial revolution' on YouTube, you'll find several five- to ten-minute videos explaining the era to you. It'll help you understand how many aspects of the business you will be working on have been shaped.

Explore!

Ever wondered why luxury goods cost so much? Or how certain luxury brands can get away by charging so much for so little? Would you like to find out? Read the Wikipedia entry about 'Veblen Goods'. Veblen (Thorstein Veblen) was an economist who said that luxury products are bought because they are expensive, thus decreasing the price of a product, perceived to be luxurious or exclusive can affect the sales of a product. Google terms: 'Veblen Goods' + 'Wikipedia'.

CHAPTER 7 – MONEY!

Do it!

No matter what stage of business you are in, enquiring about loan schemes at banks doesn't hurt in anyway. Can you make an appointment with your local bank branch or walk in and enquire about their business loans? Remember, however, that they may ask you questions about your business. Perhaps, it will be good to have a draft of your business plan to ensure you have a good, professional experience. There's no better way to learn about the funding opportunities out there than go out on the field and gather information!

Explore!

Look through the Government of India's resourceful and well-designed website catering exclusively for the information needs of entrepreneurs like you: www.business.gov.in. It covers the whole gamut, from starting a business to registering a company to, of course, funding. Click the 'Business Finance' link on the homepage and access the Government Schemes section. Want to get to it faster? Google 'Government + India + Schemes + Funding + Businesses'. Find the 'gov.in' site listed in the search results. This should show up at the top.

The business.gov.in site should also take you to the funding apex bodies' sites. Here they are in case you want to go directly:

www.nsic.co.in: On the homepage you will find the link to 'schemes', which will explain in detail the funding that NSIC makes available to banks for small business like yours. It even offers links to various well-known banks and you can start your search from here. In addition, the NSIC site offers other resources that you may be interested in.

SIDCO: You can reach the SIDCO site through the link on the Funding page in business.gov.in. Once again, it has various resources and information that can help you with you loan application. Further, Google terms 'SIDCO + India + Business' can lead you to various regional SIDCOs such as Kerala SIDCO, this can also give more region-specific information.

Explore!

Whether or not you have a unique business idea worthy of VC investment, understanding how VCs and PEs work will help you gain valuable insights about the fashion industry and understand the market better. If you had never heard of these words before and it sounds like Latin or Sanskrit to you, rest assured that there is nothing complicated and they work on a very simple idea of 'we give you money and we will take some of your profits'. So absolutely no need to be intimidated! Google terms: 1. 'Private Equity + India + Fashion/Fashion industry' 2. 'Venture Capital + India + Fashion/Fashion/industry'. Also read the Wikipedia entries on 'Private Equity' and 'Venture Capital' if interested.

CHAPTER 8 – YOUR CLOTHES AT A BIG STORE

Do it!

Do you live in a biggish city? Can you make a list of the designer stores in your city and visit them? If possible, make it a habit to visit at least once every two months. It's one thing to look at stuff on the Internet, it's another to actually see what is being displayed and sold every season. If you don't have access to these stores, don't fret. Go out there, check out your local muti-brand store and independent boutiques.

Explore!

Look through these links www.mywestside.com (Google 'Westside + Trend India), www.pantaloons.com (Google Pantaloons + India) and www.corporate.shoppersstop.com (Google 'shoppers stop + corporate). Can you find the contact details of the corporate office? Similarly, you may want to look through sites of Kimaya India and the Facebook Page of Ffolio Bangalore (Google 'Kimaya' + 'designer' + 'India' and Ffoliobangalore Facebook). Some stores such as Ffolio may not have a website and you can always get their details from their Facebook or Google pages.

Explore!

In the retail business, renting a small portion of an existing shop to sell products for a short period is called 'Shop-in-Shop'. Google 'Shop-in-Shop' + India? for information on how this retail selling format is catching on in the country. You should find many news articles on this. (Be sure to use the phrase Shop-in-Shop with double quotes as shown i.e. 'Shop-in-Shop' for best results).

Do it!

Can you make a list of funky cafés or cool shops owned by independent entrepreneurs in your city? Do you think they'd be open to the idea of having a pop-up store (turn to the chapter for definition) for your brand? The location you choose for the pop-up store will also depend on the kinds of clothes you design. What are the spaces that are ideal for your designs?

Explore!

Make a list of websites that sell clothes online, find as many as you can. Or up to a certain number such as fifty. Out of this list, make a list of ten sites that you really love and would love to see your designs sold on. Start with the following Google terms 'online fashion store + India'.

Explore!

If you're shopping for a Facebook e-commerce application, explore these options: Payvment, ShopTab and Voiyk (Google the names). But remember that new e-commerce applications are launched frequently. Use these suggestions as a starting point. Explore the new applications, compare and install the one that best suits your needs. Most of the applications do require a fee, however, many of them offer free trial periods. So you can absolutely try more than one and see it works for you.

CHAPTER 9 – YOUR FIRST FASHION WEEK

Do it!

Here's an exciting project idea for you. In your fashion sketchbook or journal, make a list of seasons you've read here, from Spring/Summer to Summer/Festive. Find images on Google with keyphrases like 'Spring/Summer <year of your choice>'. Download and get them printed on nice, glossy paper. Stick the pictures under the corresponding season. There! You have yourself a nice, personalized visual guide to various fashion seasons. Of course, feel free to adapt this project as convenient to you. Can't get glossy paper? Just get it on regular paper. Want to make a PDF instead of getting it in your fashion sketchbook. Sure. Have fun and learn at the same time.

Explore!

Look at the other fashion weeks in America, such as 'Miami Fashion Week' and 'San Francisco Fashion Week'. Think of a major city in that country and it has a fashion week.

Explore!

Google 'Paris Fashion Week + Top Designers + <your preferred year>' Enjoy what you find. You're likely to also see what looks were in, which designers were popular and how many of them set trends for the following years.

Explore!

Milan Fashion Week has been in the eye of a storm for hiring underage models. Google 'Milan Fashion Week + Models + Age' to know more. What is your take on this as an upcoming fashion designer? What do you think about the clothes they model?

Explore!

The organizers of London Fashion Week are great at promoting their event on the Internet. The website – www.londonfashionweek.co.uk/ – hosts hundreds of videos from the fashion week. Also, you can watch the fashion week live, thanks to live streaming on the website. See, you don't even have to go to London to get inspired!

Do it!

In addition to organizing fashion events like the fashion week, FDCI aims to help upcoming designers with other resources such as training and counselling. Be sure to subscribe to their newsletter to stay abreast with the latest in the industry and also information about the possible resources that you could benefit from. You should be able to find the 'Newsletter' tab on the home page. Here's the link once again: www.fdci.org

CHAPTER 10 – KEEP GOING! STAYING MOTIVATED IN THE SHORT-, MEDIUM- AND LONG-TERM

Explore!

Career Analyst Dan Pink's TED Talk, 'The Puzzle of Motivation' (subtitled in forty-two languages), has inspired millions of people around the world, since the first time it was released in 2009. To watch the video, Google 'Dan Pink' + Motivation + TED Talk.

ACKNOWLEDGEMENTS

I would like to thank Amrita Chowdhury of Harlequin India for the idea of 'democratizing' seemingly inaccessible careers through an informative book, so that everyone has a fair chance at an exciting profession. Thanks also to Amrita for letting me write this one. I would also like to thank Mohini Chaudhuri for her editorial support and valuable feedback.

Last but not the least, I would like to thank the fashion designers and entrepreneurs who shared their stories with me and demonstrated an interest in demystifying the field of fashion for young aspirants – JJ Valaya, Anita Dongre, Chaitanya Rao, Eina Ahluwalia, Sekuzo Sovenyi, Sohni Makkar and Tanya Sharma.